(Continued)

(Re)Imagining Content-Area Literacy Instruction

Roni Jo Draper, *Editor*

Paul Broomhead, Amy Petersen Jensen, Jeffery D. Nokes, and Daniel Siebert, *Co-Editors*

Foreword by Tom Bean

Teachers College, Columbia University
New York and London

National Writing Project
Berkeley, CA

Published simultaneously by Teachers College Press, 1234 Amsterdam Avenue, New York, NY 10027, and the National Writing Project, 2105 Bancroft Way, Berkeley, CA 94720-1042

The National Writing Project (NWP) is a professional development network of more than 200 university-based sites, serving teachers across disciplines and at all levels, early childhood through university. The NWP focuses the knowledge, expertise, and leadership of our nation's educators on sustained efforts to improve writing and learning for all learners.

Library of Congress Cataloging-in-Publication Data

(Re)imagining content-area literacy instruction / Roni Jo Draper, editor ; Paul
    Broomhead . . . [et al.], co-editors ; foreword by Tom Bean.
        p. cm. — (Language and literacy series)
    Includes bibliographical references and index.
    ISBN 978-0-8077-5126-8 (pbk. : alk. paper)
        1. Content area reading—United States. 2. Reading (Middle school)—
    United States. 3. Reading (Secondary)—United States. I. Draper, Roni Jo.
    II. Broomhead, Gordon Paul III. Title: Re-imagining content-area literacy
    instruction.
    LB1050.455.R46   2010
    428.4071'2—dc22   2010017034

ISBN 978-0-8077-5126-8 (paper)

Printed on acid-free paper
Manufactured in the United States of America

17   16   15   14   13   12   11   10   8   7   6   5   4   3   2   1

Contents

Foreword

Imagine two tourists, Sarah and Lindsey, visiting the Chicago Art Institute while in the city attending an education convention. As they work their way through the gallery exhibits they encounter surrealist artist Joan Miró's painting *Persons in the Night*. This is a doodle-like composition with two line-drawing faces, one with a large head and multiple eyes supported by a tiny body against an orange background with a purple half-moon hovering above the two characters.

Lindsay: I could do that! I don't get it, why does this kid's drawing get to be in the Chicago Art Institute?

Sarah (an art teacher at their high school): What do you see in this painting?

Lindsay (a literacy specialist): I don't see squat! It's stupid but okay, what do you see?

Sarah: Miró wanted viewers to confront the way children's drawings carry multiple meanings. You know what happens if you say to your son Todd, "That's a really nice boat you drew," and he says, "It's not a boat, it's a leaf." That's why we say "tell me about it" when our kids show us their art. Miró's paintings have multiple possible interpretations and their bright, child-like colors and animated forms make them come alive.

Lindsay: Okay, but I still think this is a pretty simple doodle.

Sarah: You should come by my art room sometime. I could use some help with some of the visual literacy things I'm trying in my class.

Lindsay: Yeah, I could do that. We have some funds to work with content-area teachers on professional development but I've avoided art, music, and drama because I really don't know much about those areas. I was a social studies teacher at my last high school so I just feel more comfortable there.

Sarah: That's okay. Come by next week. I'm interested in getting your help with some of my students.

If literacy specialists are to work effectively with content-area teachers, they need to be grounded in the particularities of disciplines like mathematics, history, music, art, and English from an insider's perspective. In *(Re)Imagining Literacy for Content-Area Classrooms*, Roni Jo Draper, Paul Broomhead, Amy Petersen Jensen, Jeffery D. Nokes, and Daniel Siebert take this call seriously and offer literacy professionals a much-needed insider's look at the multiple forms of collaboration that become possible when both experts in a content area and literacy specialists combine their talents to improve students' learning.

Following in the shadow of years of reading specialists trying to promote generic strategies that often amount to jamming a round peg into a square hole, there is a movement under way to seriously examine the particularities of what it means to become grounded in a discipline. This book will be crucial for literacy specialists truly interested in seeing how the world is viewed, constructed, and deconstructed from the perspective of mathematics, history, music, technology design, English Language Arts, and science. Each chapter features a collaborative effort combining the literacy specialist's knowledge of instructional frameworks and strategies that emerge from and support learning in a content area (e.g., Venn diagrams in history aimed at comparing and contrasting theories of how revolutions start). Vignettes in each chapter illustrate this collaborative process in action, often with inquiry projects aimed at getting students immersed in authentic activities in the field (e.g., in a technology design class, creating solutions to the problem of students arriving to class late after lining up at a single vending machine for a snack).

Each chapter offers an in-depth look into the world of a particular discipline and a sense that the sometimes disparate worlds of the literacy specialist and discipline expert can merge in the interest of students' learning. Both parties bring to the table craft knowledge that can ensure that students are not left in a sink-and-swim state as they become grounded in the discourse and discursive practices that make up the unique insiders' world of mathematics, history, music, technology and design, theatre, English Language Arts, science, and the visual arts.

This is a must-read for educators engaged in professional development efforts aimed at improving students' learning across the content areas. The editors and chapter authors are to be applauded for taking up the call to place content-area literacy squarely in the disciplines.

—Thomas W. Bean
University of Nevada, Las Vegas

CHAPTER 1

Aims and Criteria for Collaboration in Content-Area Classrooms

Roni Jo Draper, Paul Broomhead,
Amy Petersen Jensen, Daniel Siebert

Reform efforts sparked by reports like *Reading Next* (Biancarosa & Snow, 2006) and *Time to Act* (Carnegie Council on Advancing Adolescent Literacy, 2010) have motivated state and district leaders to increase their efforts with regard to reading and writing instruction for adolescents. These documents advocate for increased attention to the decoding, fluency, vocabulary, and comprehension needs of all adolescents, particularly those who struggle to read and write. Educators working from these documents have striven to organize their curricula in such a way as to promote these general literacy skills. For example, secondary schools that have organized professional learning communities (PLCs) often focus their work almost entirely on adolescents' achievement as measured by reading and writing assessments (Hargreaves, 2007). On the surface, this focus seems both reasonable and necessary; after all, we need a literate citizenry. However, as adolescents confront increasingly complex texts both in and out of school, general print literacies may not be sufficient to enable them to make sense of nuanced disciplinary representations and arguments.

We worry that current reform efforts may lead to a literacy that is too narrow to allow adolescents to fully engage in exploration, self-expression, and problem solving. While learning to read and write general print texts consisting of words, sentences, and paragraphs is essential for participation in society, it is often not enough. Participation also requires that people be steeped in ideas—ideas about the arts, the humanities, and the STEM disciplines (science, technology, engineering, and mathematics)—and have the literacy skills needed to read and write the specialized texts used to communicate and understand these ideas. Many of these ideas (as represented by a variety of specialized print and nonprint texts) and literacies are found in content-area classrooms. Consequently, content-area teachers can and should play an integral role in helping adolescents develop these literacies. This role, however, should not be to promote general print literacy by having students simply read and write general print texts to acquire content knowledge—i.e., reading and writing to learn. Instead, content-area teachers, with the help and support of literacy educators, should engage and support their students in reading and writing the full range of specialized texts typically used to create, express, negotiate, and understand disciplinary content—i.e., learning to read and write. Without these specialized literacies, students may be relegated to the position of reading and writing about what others are doing, rather than participating in the activities of creation, inquiry, expression, and problem solving.

Because students do not usually enter content-area classrooms knowing how to read and write the specialized print and nonprint texts of the various disciplines, teachers must provide literacy instruction in content-area classrooms. Providing students with the appropriate literacy instruction, however, may be extremely difficult. Often both literacy and content-area educators lack the knowledge and resources necessary to support students' development of these specialized disciplinary literacies. Furthermore, as we argue in Chapter 2, current conceptions of content-area literacy are inadequate for identifying and acknowledging the full range of texts students will encounter in the disciplines. We believe that content-area teachers and literacy specialists will need to work together to design literacy instruction that addresses both the literacy and content-learning needs of adolescents.

In this chapter we provide guidance for content-area teachers and literacy specialists as they collaborate to design this kind of instruction. First, we discuss the importance of imagination as a precursor to educational change. Then, we describe a set of common aims for adolescents that can serve as a guide for (re)imagining content-area literacy instruction. These common aims address the instructional goals of both literacy and content-area teachers, and can provide a shared focus that both groups can subscribe to as they work together to design instruction that meets adolescents' discipline-specific literacy needs. Third, we discuss the unique strengths content-area teachers and literacy specialists bring to a collaboration that works toward those common aims. Fourth, we describe a set of criteria by which content-area teachers and literacy specialists can evaluate the instructional plans they devise during their collaboration. Finally, we end the chapter with a brief description of the collaboration in which the authors of this book have participated and an introduction to the content chapters, which constitute the majority of this book.

IMAGINATION AS A PRECURSOR TO EDUCATIONAL CHANGE

We believe that change begins with imagination. Just as the composition of a poem begins with the imagination of the author, change in classroom instruction must begin with the imagination of teachers. Indeed, we worry that the rush to implement changes in classrooms will remain hindered if educators do not allocate sufficient time and space to imagine. Therefore, our position is that content-area teachers and literacy specialists must initiate reform efforts by first taking time to imagine together.

Our confidence in collaboration and imagination stems from our own participation in collaborative activities over the past 5 years. During this time the authors of this book have met frequently to discuss literacy and content instruction and to (re)imagine instruction for content-area classrooms. We, like other educators, have taken advantage of the imagination of others who have described the nature of literacy instruction for content-area classrooms (e.g., Carnegie Council on Advancing Adolescent Literacy, 2010; Cope & Kalantzis, 2000). However, we describe our work as (re)imagining because we have rethought or (re)imagined what has been written about content-area literacy instruction.

We believe that a (re)imagining of content-area literacy instruction is essential to meet adolescents' literacy needs. Generally, descriptions of content-area literacy either have focused narrowly on traditional print texts (which may be only tangentially related to the discipline) or have suggested interaction with particular disciplinary texts that is not consistent with the way in which disciplinary experts would read or write the texts (see Siebert & Draper, 2008, for a more in-depth discussion of this criticism as it relates to mathematics). Consequently, the instruction described in much of the literature surrounding content-area literacy leads simply to a general form of literacy that is meaningful and applicable only while one is engaged in the activity of "doing school." This general school literacy may be useful neither within the various disciplines nor in adolescents' lives outside of school. Therefore, we have worked to (re)imagine content-area literacy so that it truly would prepare adolescents to negotiate and create texts central to the disciplines and enable them to address the problems they confront in their roles as citizens of various communities. This book represents both our attempt to (re)imagine together and our desire to encourage others to do the same.

COMMON AIMS OF INSTRUCTION

If literacy and content-area educators are to work together to (re)imagine content-area literacy, they must develop a shared purpose. A common point of confusion that thwarts the development of a shared purpose is the perception that instruction is either literacy-driven or content-driven (Draper, Hall, Smith, & Siebert, 2005). We believe that this literacy-content dualism is artificial and a direct result of adopting a narrow definition of the terms *text* and *literacy*. In Chapter 2, we develop this idea in detail and suggest alternative definitions for these terms that resolve the dualism and result in a description of content-area literacy that meets the instructional goals of both literacy specialists and content-area teachers. Briefly, we have found it useful to define text to include all objects that are imbued with meaning, and literacy as a discipline-appropriate way of interpreting or creating a text. These definitions place texts and literacies at the heart of any content learning activity, because one cannot access content or participate in disciplinary practices without interpreting or creating objects that are used to convey and negotiate meaning. Likewise, one cannot become literate without understanding content or participating in authentic activity in which the literacies are situated. The overwhelming implication is that the goals of developing discipline-specific literacies and learning content are inextricably connected, and that instruction that aims to accomplish one of these goals must address the other as well.

Once content-area and literacy educators resolve the content-literacy dualism, they can work together to create a common set of instructional aims. These, along with the shared expanded definitions of *text* and *literacy*, represent a common ground and serve as "something to pursue" together (Greene, 2000). Pursuit of common aims enables educators to feel that what they hold as important will be realized in the classroom (e.g., the ability to read and write for literacy specialists, and an understanding of the content and the ability to participate fully in disciplinary practices for content-area teachers). A set of common aims can enable both content-area teachers and literacy specialists to contribute to (re)imagining classroom instruction for adolescents.

Common aims can be developed by starting a conversation about a strongly held shared belief. From the very beginning of our own collaborative conversations, it became clear that each member of the group was committed to providing instruction that benefited the lives of adolescents both in and out of schools. In fact, our shared commitment to empowering the learners in our classrooms kept us from dismissing one another's beliefs, values, and instructional goals, even when there appeared to be serious disagreements. The aims that we eventually developed were constructed from this shared commitment to adolescents as we collaboratively constructed a response to the following question: What are we striving to make possible in the lives of adolescents (Greene, 1973)? In keeping with our definitions of text and literacy, we constructed four instructional aims. We present them here as a possible starting point for conversations between content-area and literacy educators.

- *Adolescents acquire knowledge and skills within the discipline.* The knowledge and skills associated with the disciplines generally are outlined in national, state, and district standards and curricula. Implicit in these curricula are the literacies needed to negotiate and create disciplinary texts.
- *Adolescents engage in authentic activities within the discipline.* Authentic activities within the discipline are those used by knowers of the discipline (e.g., mathematicians, artists, historians, musicians) as they participate in the discipline.
- *Adolescents use what they have learned in legitimate and useful ways in their lives.* In order for disciplinary knowledge and skills to be of ultimate value to adolescents, the knowledge and skills must be useful to adolescents in their lives outside of school.

- *Adolescents use what they have learned to generate knowledge in a variety of settings.* Ultimately, communities, including disciplinary communities, benefit when participants can examine, evaluate, and critique the status quo and generate knowledge that will allow the communities to progress.

We argue below that these aims have the potential to help content-area teachers and literacy specialists achieve their instructional goals because they acknowledge and address what each group cares about. Furthermore, because content and literacy learning are inseparably intertwined within these aims, in order for both groups to achieve their respective instructional goals, they must recognize and address the instructional goals of the other group.

The Aims and Content-Area Teachers

The four aims above are acceptable to content-area teachers because they honor familiar disciplinary instructional and learning goals found in district, state, and national curricula and standards. While these documents vary from discipline to discipline in the specific goals for learners, they are consistent in describing instruction that allows adolescents to both learn content and develop the habits of mind associated with inquiry, problem solving, and creative activities within the disciplines. These recommendations are made with the belief that content instruction should prepare students for continued study within the discipline and for enhanced quality of life, promoting personal well-being and empowering individuals to participate in society.

At the same time, these aims also force content-area teachers to recognize the essential role that literacy plays in learning in the content areas. In order for adolescents to achieve these aims, they must acquire what literacy specialists often describe as tools' skills, or skills associated with reading and writing, to learn (see Fisher & Ivey, 2005). At the same time, they also must learn the multiple literacies that are required for participation in disciplinary activities and practices. Literacy specialists will recognize that many of these practices—reporting the results and conclusions of a scientific inquiry, performing a monologue, writing a mathematical proof, marshaling proper evidence as part of an historical argument, and reading technical schematics—clearly include literacy. These skills occur in conjunction with a variety of texts, and complete understanding or access to the content cannot occur without facility with those texts.

The Aims and Literacy Specialists

Because realizing each of the above aims requires attention to literacy instruction, literacy specialists also can embrace these aims. Like content-area teachers, literacy specialists work from district, state, and national curricula and standards to guide their work with other teachers. These documents point out that the literacy demands placed on individuals continue to increase, particularly in light of the explosion of texts and information available to people through digital media and the multiple literacies required in order to participate in modern society (Cope & Kalantzis, 2000). Likely no one can imagine the literacy demands that will face humanity in the next 40 years. Despite the enormity and imprecise nature of the task, literacy specialists seek to prepare adolescents for these increased literacy demands. Like content-area teaching, literacy instruction is promoted with the belief that it will help adolescents achieve increased competence in their personal lives and allow them to participate fully in society.

At the same time, these aims force literacy specialists to acknowledge and attend to the unique nature of each discipline when making recommendations for content-area literacy instruction. For students to learn content and participate in disciplinary practices, they must learn to read and write the specialized print and nonprint texts that are being used to create, convey, and negotiate meaning. Moreover, these texts must be written and read in discipline-appropriate ways in order for the appropriate meanings to be communicated and understood. For literacy specialists to meet the above aims, they must help adolescents become fluent in the multiliteracies found in the disciplines.

A Shared Focus

In summary, the instructional aims listed above can serve as an acceptable shared focus for both content-area teachers and literacy specialists. Not only do the above aims address the goals of both content-area teachers and literacy specialists, but they also require that both groups of educators acknowledge and address the goals of the other group. Thus, the aims simultaneously legitimize the instructional goals of both groups of educators. But perhaps more importantly, the aims acknowledge the value and importance that both groups place on helping adolescents live full lives, and show how the efforts of both groups of educators can be combined to empower adolescents. As such, we believe that they can serve as a rallying point about which content-area teachers and literacy specialists can form collaborations, or at the very least a starting point for collaborators to develop their own shared instructional aims.

UNIQUE STRENGTHS THAT CONTENT-AREA TEACHERS AND LITERACY SPECIALISTS BRING TO COLLABORATIONS

To achieve the instructional aims above, or a similar set of aims that attends to both the content and the literacy needs of adolescents, requires the expertise of both content-area teachers and literacy specialists. Content-area teachers bring expertise as individuals steeped in disciplinary discourses (Gee, 1996) as well as knowledge of disciplinary instruction. Literacy specialists bring an understanding of how to create instruction that supports adolescents as they develop their literacy skills and facility with texts. Both of these areas of expertise are explored below, as well as how educators might use them to create content-area literacy instruction.

Strengths of Content-Area Teachers

Content-area teachers are expert learners and doers in their disciplines. Most of them have completed advanced coursework and can engage in disciplinary practices with facility. As such, they have acquired a rich knowledge of the content and developed many of the literacies required for successful participation in their disciplines. Indeed, not only do content-area teachers know how to decode words like *ohm, tableau, null set, timbre, gamete, tariff,* and *stipple*—words that likely would not present decoding problems for skilled readers—they also possess sufficient disciplinary knowledge to understand or comprehend these words. Moreover, content-area teachers can use these words in conjunction with other words associated with their disciplines at appropriate times and for appropriate purposes. Without this content knowledge, decoding words actually would be useless, and knowing how to string them together to create coherent representations of ideas would be impossible. Likewise, content-area teachers know how to create and interpret a wide array of objects used to convey meaning, including paintings, schematic drawings, equations, costumes, musical performances, photographs, diagrams, and maps, to name just a few. This knowledge represents more than simply content knowledge, and is also more than just a type of general literacy knowledge. Rather, it is a form of discipline-specific literacy that allows content-area teachers to read and write specialized texts so they can participate legitimately in disciplinary activities. This content-specific literacy knowledge is precisely the knowledge that content-area teachers possess and, thus, bring to collaborations for content-area literacy instruction.

Because of content-area educators' expertise as learners, doers, and teachers in the discipline, they are uniquely positioned to make valuable contributions to collaborations with literacy specialists. They can recognize the specialized texts of the discipline and know how these texts should be read and written. They can reflect on their own reading and writing of disciplinary texts to identify important ways of interacting with texts that students should learn. This expertise places content-area teachers in a position to know if a particular literacy activity supports students' disciplinary literacy needs while remaining true to disciplinary norms and practices. In fact, literacy specialists should allow content-area teachers to pass final judgment as to whether or not a particular literacy activity is appropriate. This will reduce the risk of introducing instruction that is not congruent with the norms, practices, and literacies of the discipline. Lastly, content-area teachers are the most qualified to deliver content literacy instruction, because they are fluent in the literacies being taught and understand the content being communicated with the texts that students are learning to read and write.

Strengths of Literacy Specialists

While literacy specialists recognize that multiple literacies are required in order to negotiate and create the various texts particular to the disciplines, they likely do not know those literacies. Indeed, it is unrealistic to expect literacy specialists to be fluent in all the literacies that are found across the disciplines. In fact, because they often lack fluency in disciplinary literacies, they cannot dictate what literacy instruction should take place in content-area classrooms. Instead, literacy specialists must be prepared to develop literacy instructional activities *with* content-area teachers, rather than *for* content-area teachers. They can do this by helping content-area teachers identify disciplinary literacies and by sharing their knowledge of instructional frameworks for literacy.

To help content-area teachers identify literacies, literacy specialists can ask content-area teachers some of the following questions: What do you think about in order to make sense of this text? What do you need to know in order to create this text? What conventions do you adhere to when creating this text? What questions do you pose as a reader while interacting with this text? Often, the literacies inherent in disciplinary discourses (Gee, 1996) and practices may not appear obvious because it is not clear that those activities—solving an equation for a particular variable, preparing agar for a Petri dish, choosing and preparing media for a canvas, editing digital video, gathering and preserving historical artifacts, and so on—require participants to interact with texts. In these cases, literacy specialists can help content-area teachers identify the texts needed to carry out these practices, and then encourage content-area teachers to reflect on the accompanying literacies.

In addition to helping identify literacies, literacy specialists also can share their knowledge of literacy instructional frameworks. Literacy specialists know many literacy instructional frameworks that can serve as useful scaffolds for designing content-area literacy instruction. For example, the before–during–after framework, as described by authors like Vacca and Vacca (2008), can help content-area teachers consider ways they can prepare adolescents for negotiating and creating texts, how they can support adolescents while they negotiate and create texts, and how they can extend adolescents' thinking after negotiating and creating texts. Likewise, the instructional framework described by the New London Group (see Cope & Kalantzis, 2000) can help content-area teachers consider how they can engage adolescents in the situated practices in which texts and literacies are used, provide adolescents with overt instruction of the literacies under study, support adolescents as they strive to transform or transfer their literacy knowledge to other texts within and outside the discipline, and provide instruction that allows adolescents to critique disciplinary texts. Therefore, while literacy specialists are not in a position to prescribe instruction for content-area classrooms, they are in a position to help content-area teachers (re)imagine instruction for content-area classrooms.

CRITERIA FOR EVALUATING INSTRUCTION

Although common aims serve as a good beginning for a collaborative (re)imagining of content-area literacy, additional structure is required to ensure that the product of the collaboration is ultimately useful in meeting adolescents' literacy and content-area needs. In any collaboration, there is always the risk that participants may engage in compromise or collusion, processes that can lead to products that do not meet the needs of the collaborators or the populations they represent or serve (Reason, 1994). Criteria are needed to evaluate the products of collaboration to ensure that they achieve the initial aims. In terms of collaborations between content-area and literacy educators, we are particularly concerned that criteria be established to ensure that instructional approaches do not simply *fit* the various disciplines from the standpoint of the literacy specialist, but be found *essential* by experts within those disciplines. We suggest that the following criteria are useful in determining whether instructional ideas meet the four aims above:

Authenticity: Instructional ideas should be consistent with disciplinary norms and perspectives and promote both correct content knowledge and authentic disciplinary practices.
Literacy: Instructional ideas should enable content-area teachers to teach their students the literacies that are essential to learning content and engaging in disciplinary practices both in and out of school.

We describe below how both of these criteria must be met in order to achieve each of the four aims listed above.

At first glance, it may seem that the authenticity criterion is sufficient to ensure that both of the first two aims are met, namely, that students develop content-area knowledge and skills and that they learn to participate in disciplinary practices. Certainly instruction that is designed to promote correct disciplinary norms, perspectives, knowledge, and practices cannot help but support the first two aims. However, by itself this instruction may not be sufficient for achieving these aims. As noted earlier, in order for students to learn content and engage in disciplinary practices, they must be literate in the texts of the discipline. Moreover, while the immersive experiences in the discipline that are required by the authenticity criterion provide essential exposure to discipline-specific literacies, typically this exposure by itself is insufficient for students to develop these literacies (Gee, 1989, 2002). Consequently, these immersive experiences also must be coupled with sound instructional activities that teach learners how the texts of the discipline should be read and written. Thus, for the first two aims to be met, instructional ideas also must conform to the literacy criterion, which requires teachers to consciously teach the literacies of the discipline to their students.

On the other hand, attempting to address the first two aims without attending to the authenticity criterion is equally problematic. Educators might be tempted to ease students' struggles with learning content and participating in disciplinary activities by first teaching students to read and write the texts of the discipline *before* they are required to engage in content-area learning. There are two dangers associated with this practice. First, there is the very real possibility that learning to read and write the texts of the discipline outside of authentic disciplinary activities will lead students to develop artificial literacies that may not support, and may even prevent, students' learning in the discipline. Second, many of the literacies of the discipline are not apparent outside of disciplinary practices, because until students actually engage in disciplinary activity and learning, it is often unclear which objects are to be used as texts and how those objects must be read and written. In fact, educators may become aware of important disciplinary literacies only after they observe students struggle to engage in authentic activities that require those particular literacies. For these reasons, we believe that content-area literacy instruction must be situated within the context of authentic disciplinary activities.

As for the last two instructional aims, the authenticity and literacy criteria we describe should guide content-area teachers and literacy specialists to (re)imagine content-area instruction that empowers adolescents both in and outside of school. Indeed, this is really the purpose of these aims. The authenticity and literacy criteria ensure that adolescents experience the discipline in such a way as to enable them to use their newly acquired knowledge and literacies to solve problems and generate knowledge in new settings within the discipline. This happens, for example, when students apply their new literacies associated with literary critique to additional literary texts, or when they link what they have learned about writing mathematical explanations for multiplying fractions to their writing of explanations for solving systems of equations, or when they use ideas about the composition of a painting to help them compose a photograph. Additionally, the authenticity and literacy criteria suggest adolescents must be able to use their understandings of content and literacy outside the discipline. This occurs when students can use their knowledge of mathematics to critique scientific arguments, or when they use their understanding of history to create a compelling stage performance, or when they incorporate their understanding of visual design into their design of a building.

Moreover, creating instruction that adheres to the criteria that we have described ensures that adolescents will be prepared to use their knowledge and literacies in their lived worlds. While the lived worlds of adolescents certainly include their futures after schooling, they also include students' immediate out-of-school lives. It may be a challenge, for example, to demonstrate how adolescents might use their new understandings of molecular bonding outside of school settings, even though science teachers agree to its importance. However, authentic practice dictates that science teachers engage adolescents in critical discussions about how their community responds to chemical spills, because this is also central to scientific discourses. Moreover, engaging in those discussions requires particular literacy skills, skills that are best developed in science classrooms. Ultimately, teachers must assist adolescents in using their newly acquired literacies as part of authentic practices surrounding understanding, critiquing, and challenging the status quo, both within the disciplines and within society. This requires teachers to support adolescents as they question and critique the texts they encounter in the classroom and outside the classroom, and develop skills that allow them to create their own texts—texts that represent adolescents' imaginations of a better world.

We recognize that our aims are lofty and our criteria challenging to meet. Some might even say they are too idealistic and unattainable. However, we feel these aims and criteria, or similar aims and criteria that acknowledge and address the content and literacy needs of adolescents, must guide our work together as educators if we hope to prepare adolescents with the knowledge, skills, and dispositions they need to participate fully in the various communities in which they find themselves and to make those communities better (Dewey, 1916). Collaboration between content-area teachers and literacy specialists offers the most hope in achieving these instructional aims.

AN INTRODUCTION TO (RE)IMAGINING LITERACIES FOR CONTENT-AREA CLASSROOMS

The remainder of this chapter serves as an introduction to the book. We describe our own collaboration, which has made this book possible, followed by a brief introduction to the content chapters.

Our Collaboration

The various authors in this book have been involved in collaborative activities as members of the Brigham Young University Literacy Study Group (BYU LSG). Our (re)imagining occurred as we read and discussed the literature surrounding content-area literacy and wondered aloud what instruction might look like that supports both content and literacy learning. We have interrogated one another and have listened patiently to one another as we have struggled to articulate burgeoning ideas. These discussions continued until the ideas met the criteria we have outlined here.

In fact, this book represents a collaborative effort and our (re)imagining of literacies for content-area classrooms. The framing chapters (Chapters 1, 2, and 11) are authored by the various book editors. The ideas presented in these framing chapters represent the ideas that developed over the course of our collaboration. The authors collaborated in writing the chapters (serving as equal authors) and checked their ideas with the other members of the BYU LSG, to ensure that the ideas presented were truly representative of the ideas that grew out of the collaboration.

Content-area educators who have participated in our collaboration (some of whom also served as book editors) wrote the remaining chapters of the book. Everyone has carefully explored the habits of mind and creative activity associated with literacy and inquiry in the given area of study. This exploration has occurred as each of them has engaged in study of the discipline along with the pedagogy associated with the discipline. Experiences associated with teaching in public school settings, preparing preservice teachers in the university setting, and continued conversations with classroom teachers have provided each of the authors with significant time in educational settings where discipline-specific content was taught and/or discussed. Indeed, the authors have thought deeply about the ways in which educators might help adolescents to negotiate and create print and nonprint texts. These experiences have supported all of the writers as they have worked to (re)imagine instruction for adolescents in their disciplines that is designed to realize the aims we have described here.

Finally, each chapter has been read by all the participants and discussed at collaboration meetings of the BYU LSG. These group discussions provided authors with ideas for revisions to their chapters. The chapter authors also have worked directly with one of the book editors to refine ideas, sharpen arguments, and ensure that the ideas presented across the chapters are coherent without being overly redundant.

Introduction to the Content Chapters

The intent of each content chapter is to illustrate what literacy instruction might look like within the specific disciplines without being prescriptive. The use of vignettes throughout the chapters represents (re)imagined content-area classrooms from the perspectives of the authors. In fact, the contexts of the vignettes—the teachers, students, and interactions—were drawn from the imaginations of the authors as they considered what instruction that promotes both content and literacy learning can look like. In most cases the instructional units described in the vignettes represent a (re)imagining of units they have created and used with adolescents to learn content that now reflect a mindful attention to literacy. We will highlight here some of the ways in which the authors illustrate how content-area teachers—with assistance from literacy specialists—can help adolescents achieve the aims we have described in this chapter.

The authors demonstrate how content-area teachers can support adolescents as they acquire knowledge and skills within the disciplines—our first instructional aim. Indeed, they describe literacy instruction for content-area classrooms that more fully supports students' comprehensive understanding of the discipline. For example, Siebert and Hendrickson illustrate how content instruction is incomplete without thoughtful consideration and implementation of the multiple literacies in mathematics classrooms. In fact, they make it clear that literacy and content are inextricably linked in such a way that when mathematics teachers attend to the multiple literacies required in order to learn, communicate, and participate in mathematics, they help students understand the nature of mathematics. Similarly, Nokes describes history teaching that attends keenly to discipline-specific literacies. He asserts that by identifying history-specific literacy strategies, educators can help adolescents think and read like historians. Additionally, Nokes emphasizes the necessity of implementing both explicit and implicit literacy instruction to help students engage in authentic historical inquiry experiences. By doing so, history teachers can help their students learn history as they acquire the skills used to negotiate and create historical texts.

The authors also illustrate the second aim we describe—that adolescents engage in authentic disciplinary activities. For example, Broomhead declares that while music classrooms are primarily nonprint spaces, they are text-rich environments nonetheless. He encourages music educators to explore the variety of texts and their accompanying literacies available within music classrooms. By so doing, music educators can engage adolescents in the full range of musical interactions, rather than continue to focus narrowly on performance literacies. Likewise, Shumway and Wright demonstrate how literacy instruction can be infused into the technology design cycle to better engage students in the design process. They demonstrate how teaching the multiple literacies associated with technology allows adolescents access to the design cycle and how engaging in the design cycle provides a legitimate purpose for adolescents to engage with a variety of technology texts. Furthermore, they contend that technology teachers can provide rich opportunities for helping adolescents develop print and nonprint literacies essential to participating in genuine technology processes in secondary classrooms.

Another purpose of the content chapters is to demonstrate that teachers must help adolescents use what they have learned in legitimate and useful ways in their lives—our third instructional aim. Jensen does this by suggesting that theatre teachers (re)imagine ways that literacy instruction can provide students with the tools to respond purposefully to both written and performed texts in theatre classrooms. Jensen demonstrates that by focusing literacy instruction on the modes of inquiry particular to theatre, teachers can help adolescents acquire a range of literacies that can be immediately useful in their lives outside of school. She advocates perspective-taking and contextualization for deep disciplinary understanding that has the potential to help adolescents make sense of human activity in general and their own lives in particular.

Continuing a focus on the human experience, Grierson and Nokes describe English language arts (ELA) instruction that allows adolescents to use their literacies in legitimate ways in their immediate lives. They point out that while all ELA teachers may not have a strong background in or inclination toward literacy instruction, they generally seek to engage adolescents in literature that can help them understand the human condition and make sense of their lived worlds. The authors describe how ELA teachers can combine comprehension strategy instruction and a process approach with an expanded view of the literary canon that relates to adolescents' lives outside of school. In this way, ELA teachers can provide access to a range of important literary texts.

Finally, in keeping with the fourth instructional aim, the authors of the content chapters describe content-area classrooms in which adolescents use what they have learned to generate knowledge in a variety of settings. For instance, Draper and Adair describe a unit of instruction that allows adolescents to generate knowledge about organisms by comparing and contrasting a range of issues related to a particular pair of organisms and the environments in which they live. Draper and Adair suggest that adolescents use various scientific literacies to generate knowledge in the same way as they are used by scientists—namely, generating questions, performing careful observations, collecting and analyzing data, and creating viable scientific arguments. Similarly, Jensen, Asay, and Gray describe how students in visual arts can use their multiple literacies to generate ideas about visual culture and expression. In this way, they, along with the other content authors, challenge notions of what counts as knowledge for the various disciplines.

Each chapter represents our own first steps at (re)imagining content-area literacy instruction. The vignettes that we include in the various chapters represent a fusion of both excellent content instruction and our own (re)imagining of those classrooms when literacy instruction has been infused into the curriculum. Our (re)imagining is grounded in the belief that all educators can be, should be, and probably are to some degree already literacy educators.

Ultimately, we suggest a process of investigating content-specific literacies. We realize that identification of the multiple literacies associated with the range of texts central to the disciplines continues to expand though technologies, increased access, and creativity. Our own process of engagement and recognition of the variety and potential of crucial content-area texts, and the new literacies that are required in order to fully comprehend and employ them, has come through collaborative effort and investigation. We have enjoyed the difference that discussions of literacy have made in our own understandings of the disciplines and disciplinary instruction, and we invite you into our circle of collaboration in hopes that you might benefit from a new way of looking at the things you are already skilled at and, more important, how you might do things even better.

Authors' note: The authors of this chapter contributed equally to its authorship.

REFERENCES

Biancarosa, G., & Snow, C. E. (2006). *Reading next: A vision for action and research in middle and high school literacy* (2nd ed.). New York: Carnegie Corporation.

Carnegie Council on Advancing Adolescent Literacy. (2010). *Time to act: An agenda for advancing adolescent literacy for college and career success.* New York: Carnegie Corporation.

Cope, B., & Kalantzis, M. (Eds.). (2000). *Multiliteracies: Literacy learning and the design of social futures.* New York: Routledge.

Dewey, J. (1916). *Democracy and education: An introduction to the philosophy of education.* New York: Free Press.

Draper, R. J., Hall, K. M., Smith, L. K., & Siebert, D. (2005). What's more important—literacy or content? Confronting the literacy–content dualism. *Action in Teacher Education, 27*(2), 12–21.

Fisher, D., & Ivey, G. (2005). Literacy and language as learning in content-area classes: A departure from "every teacher a teacher of reading." *Action in Teacher Education, 27*(2), 3–11.

Gee, J. P. (1989). What is literacy? *Journal of Education, 171*(1), 18–25.

Gee, J. P. (1996). *Social linguistics and literacies: Ideology in discourses* (2nd ed.). London: RoutledgeFalmer.

Gee, J. P. (2002). Learning in semiotic domains: A social and situated account. In D. L. Schallert, C. M. Fairbanks, J. Worthy, B. Maloch, & J. V. Hoffman (Eds.), *51st yearbook of the National Reading Conference* (pp. 23–32). Oak Creek, WI: National Reading Conference.

Greene, M. (1973). *Teacher as stranger*. New York: Wadsworth.

Greene, M. (2000). Imagining futures: The public school and possibility. *Journal of Curriculum Studies, 32*(2), 267–280.

Hargreaves, A. (2007). Sustainable professional learning communities. In L. Stoll & K. S. Louis (Eds.), *Professional learning communities: Divergence, depth and dilemmas* (pp. 181–195). London: Open University Press.

Reason, P. (1994). Three approaches to participative inquiry. In N. K. Denzin & Y. S. Lincoln (Eds.), *Handbook of qualitative research* (pp. 324–339). Thousand Oaks, CA: Sage.

Siebert, D., & Draper, R. J. (2008). Why content-area literacy messages do not speak to mathematics teachers: A critical content analysis. *Literacy Research and Instruction, 47,* 229–245.

Vacca, R. T., & Vacca, J. A. (2008). *Content area reading: Literacy and learning across the curriculum* (9th ed.). Boston: Allyn & Bacon.

CHAPTER 2

Rethinking Texts, Literacies, and Literacy Across the Curriculum

Roni Jo Draper
Daniel Siebert

The call for every content-area teacher to be a literacy teacher is not a new idea. Nevertheless, despite persuasive and continued appeals for literacy across the curriculum, often content-area teachers still remain resistant to implementing reading and writing instruction in their classrooms. In our own experiences as teacher educators, we have encountered many situations where there is conflict between literacy advocates and content-area teachers. The following are just a few examples:

> *Situation 1*: A music teacher informs a literacy coach that he is willing to teach reading in his classroom when the English teacher starts teaching the circle of fifths.
> *Situation 2*: A mathematics teacher complains to colleagues about being required by school administrators to have her students Drop Everything And Read (DEAR) in fourth period, causing her to lose 15 minutes of instructional time.
> *Situation 3*: A literacy specialist receives icy stares from physical education teachers throughout her literacy presentation to faculty at a local high school.
> *Situation 4*: A technology teacher checks literacy off his to-do list after placing copies of *Popular Mechanics* on a shelf in the back of his classroom.

Even when some type of compromise is made between literacy advocates and content-area teachers, the result is often unsatisfactory to one or both parties, as the second and fourth situations above illustrate.

The conflicts that arise between literacy advocates and content-area specialists often leave both groups pointing fingers at each other. Literacy specialists frequently perceive uncooperative content-area teachers as resistant, unmotivated, unimaginative, or uncaring. Even worse, content-area teachers sometimes are depicted as self-serving defenders of artificial boundaries between bodies of knowledge, boundaries that enhance their status and enable them to lay claim to important resources. On the other hand, frustrated content-area specialists may describe literacy advocates as naïve, meddling, and ignorant of content-area goals. Indeed, content-area teachers may perceive that the literacy practices described and defended by literacy advocates have been designed only to meet literacy goals without similar attention to content goals.

Closer to the truth is that both literacy advocates and content-area specialists are strongly motivated by their concerns for adolescents. Literacy advocates are attuned to the multiple literacies required to function in society and are committed to helping students develop fluency with these literacies. In contrast, content-area specialists are concerned about the content knowledge, skills, and practices that adolescents will need to function in an increasingly specialized and technical society. While these two perspectives are not necessarily contradictory, the difference in focus nonetheless can lead to conflicts that appear difficult to resolve.

The many instructional strategies promoted by literacy advocates as useful for teaching reading and writing across the curriculum have done little to resolve these conflicts. Research has shown that general literacy strategies or study skills taught in isolation of content do little to help students read and write in the content areas (e.g., Bean, 2000). Furthermore, when literacy advocates have pushed for content-area teachers to use these strategies in their classes, many of the teachers have balked, claiming that they lack the time and expertise to teach reading and writing, and that such teaching should be left to the language arts teachers (Alvermann & Moore, 1991; Stewart & O'Brien, 1989). To be fair, many content-area teachers have received little instruction in how to adapt general literacy strategies to their specific content areas. For example, we have noted that many of the literacy messages addressed to mathematics teachers misrepresent the nature of the discipline and ignore the influence of the discipline on what counts as text, reading, and writing (Siebert & Draper, 2008). The fact that many content-area teachers do not use general literacy instructional strategies may indicate not only that they do not know how to use these strategies, but also that these strategies fit poorly with the content-area goals of the teachers and the discipline-specific literacy practices in those content areas (Conley, 2008).

To avoid these conflicts over the teaching of literacy, some literacy educators have shifted to advocating the use of reading and writing to learn in the content areas (e.g., Fisher & Ivey, 2005). No longer pushed to *teach* reading and writing, content-area teachers are encouraged instead to *use* reading and writing as a way to teach the content they want students to learn. This exposure to and practice in reading and writing in the content areas seems to be a reasonable approach for helping adolescents improve their reading and writing skills while also increasing their knowledge of the content. Thus, this approach seems to address the needs of both literacy advocates and content-area educators.

Unfortunately, the practice of reading and writing to learn in the content areas has yet to meet the expectations of literacy and content-area educators. Research on writing as a tool for learning has yielded mixed results, leaving many questions about just how useful it is for learning content (Ackerman, 1993; Bangert-Downs, Hurley, & Wilkinson, 2004). Reading for content knowledge also can be problematic, because often there are other methods that are preferred in the content areas for acquiring skills, knowledge, and dispositions. For example, in science education, the inquiry process is valued over reading as a means for producing scientific knowledge (National Research Council, 1996, 2000). For many content specialists, reading about the discipline is not the same as, and is often less valued than, participating in the practices of the discipline. Furthermore, many of these practices do not entail reading *per se* in that students engaged in these practices are not reading printed texts consisting of words, sentences, and paragraphs, but rather are negotiating different kinds of representations of content in different ways. Consequently, the practice of reading and writing to learn is of limited value to content-area teachers, and thus does not resolve basic tensions between literacy and content-area teachers.

Because the conflicts between literacy specialists and content-area teachers are caused in part by their differing goals, resolution of these conflicts cannot occur until both groups of educators find common ground on which to base their goals. We believe that the key to finding common ground is to rethink literacy instruction using broadened definitions of *text* and *literacy*. To demonstrate this, we examine different meanings of the terms, discuss their implications for literacy instruction in content-area classrooms, and demonstrate why broadened definitions of *text* and *literacy* can help content-area teachers and literacy specialists bridge differences and create a fruitful working relationship.

TRADITIONAL VIEWS OF *TEXT* AND *LITERACY*

The meanings of the terms *text* and *literacy* often seem so universally understood that speakers frequently use them without providing definitions. In the context of discussions about literacy instruction, the term *text* typically is taken to mean written or printed words, sentences, and paragraphs. Based on this definition, examples of texts might include textbooks, trade books, worksheets, and notes. The term *literacy* usually is taken to mean fluency in reading and writing these print texts. Thus, literacy in a particular discipline is equated with being able to read and write printed materials that are composed of words, sentences, and paragraphs, and that address the content of the particular subject area.

It is not surprising that these are the most common understandings of the terms *text* and *literacy*, because historically these are the meanings that speakers and authors have associated with these terms in the context of discussing reading and writing across the curriculum. In perhaps the earliest call for reading instruction across the curriculum, Gray (1925) stated, "Each teacher who makes reading assignments is responsible for the direction and supervision of the reading and study activities that are involved" (p. 71). Underlying this call for literacy instruction is the identification of text with printed words. A similar meaning is evident in more recent calls for literacy instruction. For example, McKenna and Robinson (1990) claim that "students' understanding of the content presented in all subjects could be substantially enhanced through appropriate writing assignments or through supplemental reading" (p. 185). Vacca (2002) suggests that "content area teachers can make a difference in the school lives of adolescents when they incorporate reading strategy minilessons into their instructional repertoire" (p. 184). Even when literacy educators define text to include more than just printed words, they seldom address literacy involving nontraditional texts, which does little to challenge the predominant view of text consisting solely of words.

Although the definitions above may be the most common for the terms *text* and *literacy*, they may not be the most useful for conceptualizing literacy instruction in the content areas. In fact, there are at least three major problems that can arise from using these meanings when discussing, designing, and implementing content-area literacy instruction. First, literacy specialists may overlook many of the literacy events that are already present in the classroom. Second, content-area teachers may fail to notice literacy processes that are integral to learning and engaging in disciplinary activities. Third, when literacy instruction is limited to facilitating fluency with printed words, conflicts can arise between literacy and content-area learning goals. To illustrate these three problems, consider the following situation in an algebra classroom:

Vignette: Ms. Baker wants her algebra students to understand how the different numbers in the equation of a line influence the graph of a line. Starting with the slope-intercept form of the line, $y = mx + b$, she has students substitute different numbers for m and b to see what effect changing these numbers has on the graph of the line. She has her students work in pairs using graphing calculators to graph the lines. After her students experiment with several different values for m and b, Ms. Baker asks the students to make conjectures about how the values of m and b affect the graph of a line, and to be prepared to share these conjectures verbally with the class.

Ms. Santana, the school's literacy specialist, is observing the lesson. She admires Ms. Baker's creativity and the level of engagement in which the students seemed involved with the lesson, as well as the understanding the students seem to be developing. But she also feels the same concern that she often feels when she visits a mathematics class, namely, that there is no reading or writing of traditional print materials, and thus no literacy instruction happening. She needs to talk to Ms. Baker about this.

To Ms. Santana, this particular mathematics lesson does not seem to involve literacy. After all, there are no printed words, sentences, or paragraphs for students to read or write. However, students are engaged in the process of making sense of a very important mathematical object, namely, the slope-intercept equation of a line. Furthermore, the goal of the lesson seems to be to help the students understand that the graph of a line will be determined by which numbers appear in the slope-intercept equation of the line. If the lesson is successful, students should be able to *read* a slope-intercept equation and know exactly how the graph of the line should look. They also should be able to look at the graph of a line and *write* a slope-intercept equation for that line. In a sense, then, Ms. Baker actually is engaging in literacy instruction to help her students learn how to become literate with slope-intercept equations of lines. Ms. Santana, who is looking for students to use traditional print texts, fails to observe any literacy events in Ms. Baker's classroom. This illustrates the first problem of using traditional definitions of text and literacy: Literacy educators may miss important literacy events, and perhaps even excellent literacy instruction, in content-area classrooms if they look only for the reading and writing of printed words, sentences, and paragraphs.

The second problem that arises from using traditional definitions of text and literacy is that content-area teachers may not recognize important literacy events in their instruction. In the above example, Ms. Baker does recognize that students need to learn how to read and write slope-intercept equations for lines. However, she may not be aware that students may have difficulty *reading* the calculator-generated graphs. For Ms. Baker, it is obvious from the graphs of the lines exactly what aspects of the lines have changed due to changes in the numbers. Her students, however, may not know which features they should attend to while making sense of a graph. For example, for students to make the appropriate connection between the equation and the graph, they must attend to the point at which the line crosses the y-axis (the major vertical axis on the graph). Many of her students will not know this and instead will focus their attention to where the line crosses the x-axis (the major horizontal axis on the graph). They then will be unable to connect the equation of the line to its graph. For this instructional activity to be successful, Ms. Baker must recognize the literacy event of reading graphs and help her students learn how to do this.

The third problem that arises from the use of traditional definitions of text and literacy is that it can lead directly to conflicts between literacy specialists and content-area teachers. As noted before, Ms. Santana sees no literacy instruction taking place because students are not reading or writing printed words in sentences and paragraphs. To alleviate this problem, Ms. Santana most likely will suggest introducing traditional print material into the lesson so that Ms. Baker can engage in literacy instruction. For example, Ms. Santana might recommend having the students read the textbook section on linear equations or historical accounts of the development of linear equations. For writing activities, she might suggest that students describe the process they engaged in during class or write a poem about linear equations. These suggestions, however, may not appeal to Ms. Baker. She may feel that the additional understanding and competency these literacy activities might foster in her students do not warrant expending additional class time. Unlike the literacy specialist, Ms. Baker may not see any need for the introduction of these traditional print texts in order to achieve her content instruction goals. And even if she were to concede the need for additional instruction on linear equations, Ms. Baker might not be convinced that having students work with traditional print texts is the most productive approach. Ms. Santana and Ms. Baker have a serious conflict of goals, which is likely to lead to an irresolvable disagreement over Ms. Baker's instruction. Finding a way to work through these conflicts has the potential to improve Ms. Baker's instruction and ultimately help students construct more powerful conceptions of mathematics.

The use of traditional definitions of text and literacy may be responsible for the majority of conflicts between literacy specialists and content-area teachers. In order to address literacy, the literacy specialist feels compelled to make recommendations that include the reading or writing of traditional print text. Furthermore, the literacy specialist is unlikely to consider alternative instruction that does not involve traditional print materials. The literacy specialist's commitment to improving literacy, as she understands it, may cause her to place greater value on the inclusion of traditional print material in instruction than on the students' content-area learning. On the other hand, the content-area teacher has a limited amount of time to devote to each idea or topic. Any instructional recommendation that she receives that costs class time but does not yield a commensurate return in improved content-area understanding or competency will likely be judged as an intrusion upon her class. Content-area teachers are likely to resist the inclusion of traditional print materials if there are more effective ways to increase students' content learning. Simply stated, when literacy is defined as fluency with traditional print materials, the instructional goals of literacy specialists and content-area teachers do not match up, and may even be in direct conflict with each other. Small wonder, then, that conflicts frequently arise between the two groups of educators.

REDEFINING *TEXT* AND *LITERACY*

Because of the issues raised above, it may be time to explore different definitions of *text* and *literacy*. This may offend some educators, given the prominent place traditional definitions have occupied for years in the field of content-area literacy. Nevertheless, educators and researchers interested in literacy have already begun to rethink these definitions. In particular, scholars have noted that multimodal materials, particularly content from the Internet, have become an important part of adolescents' lives both in and out of school. This has caused some researchers to argue that the definition of text must be expanded to include nonprint, pictures, and audio content so as to acknowledge and address the changing literate practices of adolescents who are increasingly engaged in activities associated with a variety of media (Bean, Bean, & Bean, 2001; Cope & Kalantzis, 2000). In addition, content-area specialists have argued that the definition of text should be expanded to include important inscriptions or objects that students use to express, understand, and learn content knowledge and skills (Draper & Siebert, 2004; Norris & Phillips, 2003). Thus, efforts have already begun to be made to rethink definitions for text.

The traditional definition of literacy also is being questioned. Gee (2001) argues that "what is relevant to learning literacy is not English in general, but specific varieties of English" (p. 714). Gee's point is that what counts as correct literate behavior depends on the social context in which that behavior is situated. This reasoning makes sense when considering the particular natures of the different content areas. Because each discipline has distinct ways of engaging in inquiry, marshaling evidence, and expressing findings and ideas, each discipline has a unique way of reading, writing, speaking, and acting—in other words, a particular literacy. This has led scholars to suggest that instead of trying to foster literacy in general, educators should focus instead on fostering specific literacies, particularly those literacies that would help adolescents to function in society and live rich work, public, and private lives (Cope & Kalantzis, 2000). This multiliteracies perspective is further supported by research that has studied students' literate activities in and out of the classroom and documented the multiple literacies that constitute adolescents' complex lives (Bean et al., 2001; Moje, Overby, Tysvaer, & Morris, 2008).

Redefining Texts

Although scholars have begun to challenge the traditional definitions of *text* and *literacy*, they have not reached consensus about what the new definitions should be. As the contributors to this book considered what definitions to adopt for *text* and *literacy*, we were influenced both by the work cited above and by our attempts to avoid the problems that are caused by the traditional definitions. We knew that our definition of text should allow us to recognize the text-like objects from different disciplines that students must engage with in a "literate" way, where literate is understood loosely to include making sense of (i.e., "reading") and producing in a meaningful way (i.e., "writing"). For us, these text-like objects included such things as a verbal explanation in a mathematics class, a painting in an art class, a conductor's movements in a music class, a defensive basketball formation in a physical education class, a play script in a drama class, a pattern in a sewing class, a timeline in a history class, a graduated cylinder in a science class, and a short story in a language arts class, to name but a few. Each of these objects, and many more like them, are the essential objects that students must make use of in order to develop content-area expertise.

To include all of the objects whose use seems to involve a literate activity, we needed a general, broad definition for text. We eventually adopted the following definition: A *text* is any representational resource (Cope & Kalantzis, 2000) or object that people intentionally imbue with meaning, in the way they either create or attend to the object, to achieve a particular purpose. Our definition of text allows for objects that can be attended to through any combination of the five senses. Furthermore, a text does not have to be permanent, like a written sentence. Instead, it can be as fleeting as a live dance performance, the motion of a conductor's gestures, or the colors of a liquid during a chemical reaction. This definition of text suggests that the meaning of a text is never set in stone. Instead, meanings are determined by the purposes of those who write and/or read a particular text. These purposes, in turn, are influenced by the backgrounds of the readers and writers and the contexts in which they and the texts are situated.

A broadened definition of text can help educators avoid the three problems associated with a traditional definition. First, because texts include all of the objects with which people make meaning, every content-area classroom is a text-rich environment. Rather than insist on traditional print materials being infused into the instruction, literacy specialists can focus instead on the texts used to help students learn content. As they do so, they may no longer overlook important literacy activities that are occurring in content-area classrooms, or the literacy instruction that content-area teachers might already be providing for their students. Second, a broadened view of text can alert content teachers to attend to all the objects that they and their students use to make meaning. The broad definition of text captures all of the objects that students need to make sense of in order to gain content knowledge and expertise. By attending to all texts, and not just printed words, content-area teachers can focus on all of the literacy activities that directly influence their students' content-area learning.

Last, a broadened view of text can significantly reduce the conflicts between content-area teachers and literacy specialists by aligning their instructional goals so that these goals are no longer at odds. If content-area teachers come to see all of the objects that they and their students imbue with meaning as texts, they will begin to recognize that all disciplinary teaching and learning involve heavy text use. Moreover, unless students become fluent in reading and writing these texts, they will be unable to learn the content matter. Consequently, a broadened notion of text implies that content-area literacy instruction is a vital, everyday concern of content-area teachers. A broadened definition of text also can change literacy specialists' view of content-area literacy. Instead of insisting on the inclusion of traditional print material in lessons so that literacy instruction can take place, literacy specialists can direct content-area teachers' attention to texts that are already being used in the classroom and assist them in helping their students develop fluency with these texts. Simply put, a broadened definition of text realigns the instructional goals of content-area teachers and literacy specialists, making them compatible and complementary. It is key to resolving conflicts between the two groups of educators.

Redefining Literacy

An expanded definition of *text* necessitates an expanded definition of *literacy*. The term *literacy* has been used in two distinct ways. First, in its most fundamental sense, literacy traditionally has been defined as the ability to read and write. Second, literacy has been used to describe knowledge of a domain (as in computer literacy or science literacy). We have adopted a definition of literacy that combines both of these notions. We acknowledge that in order to successfully read or write a text, an individual must possess both the ability to read and write *and* the conceptual or disciplinary understanding or knowledge that makes up the content of the text. Because reading and writing play such a prominent role in defining literacy, a discussion of these terms must precede a further discussion of literacy.

It should be clear that our expanded definitions of texts and literacies also necessitate an expanded view of *reading* and *writing*. Generally, reading and writing are considered meaning-making or meaning-representing practices (Ruddell, 2005). However, like the other terms associated with literacy, these practices have been associated primarily with print texts. As such, individuals, including educators, typically have not considered reading as a practice done in conjunction with nonprint texts such as film, music, sculptures, graphs, manipulatives, graduated cylinders, or riverbanks. Instead, words such as *viewing* or *listening* have been used to mark the meaning-making practices done with nonprint texts. Likewise, educators don't often speak of writing in conjunction with a stage performance, painting, creating a graph, creating a Web page, or making a speech. Rather, ways of representing meaning or ideas have been denoted by terms like *producing* or *speaking*. Because reading and writing continue to denote practices done with traditional print texts, we have adopted the terms *negotiating* (for reading) and *creating* (for writing) for the meaning-making or meaning-representing practices done by individuals as they interact with or create texts.

We return now to our definition of literacy. *Literacy* is the ability to negotiate (e.g., read, view, listen, taste, smell, critique) and create (e.g., write, produce, sing, act, speak) texts in discipline-appropriate ways or in ways that other members of a discipline (e.g., mathematicians, historians, artists) would recognize as "correct" or "viable." The inclusion of discipline-appropriateness in our definition of literacy acknowledges that interacting (i.e., negotiating and creating) with texts in meaningful ways requires knowledge of the content and processes associated with disciplinary domains such as mathematics, science, visual arts, music, literature, engineering, dance, and history. Therefore, to be considered literate in theatre, for example, means to be able to negotiate, create, and critique theatre texts in theatre-appropriate ways. As such, an actor might read a play text in order to determine the objectives and possible tactics of a character in preparation for depicting that character on stage. Furthermore, this reading may be very different from how a literary critic might read the same play text; certainly, the reading will result in the writing of different texts—for the actor, the resulting text is a stage performance; for the literary critic, the resulting text may be a traditional print text.

To further illustrate the influence of the discipline on what counts as literacy, consider how the following five texts might be used in a classroom: a banana peel; a Honey Bunches of Oats® cereal box; a receipt from a home-improvement store; a cream-colored, hand-addressed envelope; and a yellow-and-blue-striped mug with a missing handle. These texts, chosen from a garbage sack, require a different kind of reading—and thus literacy—depending on the discipline from which one reads them. Imagine that a history teacher brings them into her classroom. A history teacher would help students to wonder what the cereal box, along with the other objects, might reveal about the individual(s) who discarded them or about the society in which such objects exist. She might ask her students: What was purchased at the store and when? Who sent the envelope and to whom? Can any inferences be made about the contents of the envelope, even in their absence? However, imagine that the same texts are used by an art teacher. The questions he would use to guide his students' reading of the texts would likely be quite different: What possible meanings can we gather from the image, colors, layout, design, and symmetry found on the cereal box or the discarded mug based on our understanding of visual culture? What feelings might be evoked by the texture of the cream-colored envelope?

The differences in the reading of the same texts by individuals from various disciplines can be subtle. Our definition of literacy acknowledges those differences. Furthermore, it acknowledges that many of the differences in reading and writing can be attributed to the traditions, conventions, and purposes that distinguish participation within various disciplines.

INSTRUCTIONAL IMPLICATIONS
FOR BROAD DEFINITIONS OF TEXT AND LITERACY

Adopting this expanded definition of literacy has several implications. Our first implication is that what counts as text and the ways texts are used (i.e., negotiated and created) are determined largely by the discipline. Indeed, the work of historians involves examining artifacts and print material in order to make inferences about historical events or how people lived. In this case all of the objects retrieved from the trash are legitimate historical texts that must be read in particular ways, if one is said to be doing history. Furthermore, the reading of those texts will result in additional texts—history—that must be written in ways that historians would recognize as history. However, the garbage texts, in and of themselves, may be of less consequence for a mathematician. While a mathematician certainly could measure and perform computations based on the objects found in the trash, it is less likely that a mathematician would use these texts as central objects of investigation. Likewise, an artist might find the broken mug more central to his or her work as an artist than a receipt from a home-improvement store.

Therefore, what counts as text and literacy within the various disciplines is determined by the individuals who make up the disciplines: historians, artists, scientists, actors, mathematicians. These determinations, therefore, often are socially, politically, and economically motivated. However, despite how the literacies came about, it is simply the case that texts must be read and written differently depending on the discipline in which they are being used or created. For example, mathematics texts often are created to justify mathematical conclusions. Thus, these texts are read by other mathematicians to determine whether the justification is sound. Meanwhile, historians create texts to describe a historical event or time. These descriptions are based on observations and inferences from other texts and are read by other historians to determine whether the available evidence supports the inferences drawn. While these discipline-specific literacies may appear to have only subtle differences, they are differences nonetheless, and helping adolescents to acquire and learn these literacies is a vital aspect of content-area instruction.

This leads to the next instructional implication for an expanded definition of literacy. Literacy instruction in content-area classrooms must focus on the texts and literacies central to the discipline. Disciplines are defined by the texts and the literacies used to negotiate, create, and critique those texts. Accordingly, the further away content-area instruction is from the texts and literacies central to a discipline, the less the instruction is focused on the content and processes recognized as legitimate for the discipline.

Consider the following texts: a report of a recent medical discovery found at www.nytimes.com (the online version of the *New York Times*), a chemist's lab notes, a haiku describing the water cycle, the Periodic Table of the Elements, a display about indigenous rodents at the local natural history museum, a rap song about planets, an article about sand found in *Scientific American*, a presentation made by a biologist at a research conference, and a children's storybook about the icky sticky frog (Bentley, 2008). All of these texts include some level of science content and can be placed on a continuum from more scientific to less scientific. The most scientific texts, or the texts that are more closely related to day-to-day participation as a scientist, would include the Periodic Table of the Elements, the chemist's lab notes, and the presentation by the biologist at a research conference because these represent legitimate texts used and created by scientists as a natural part of their work as scientists. The less scientific texts would be the haiku, the rap, and the children's storybook. Indeed, scientists do not create these kinds of texts to share with other scientists as a part of their work or as part of legitimate participation within the discipline of science. The other texts—the *Times* report, the rat display, and the sand article—fall somewhere between the two extremes. We recommend, then, that content-area teachers focus their teaching on the texts and literacies that fall closer to the end of the continuum that represents the discipline. This does not mean that texts like haikus, rap songs, or children's storybooks have no place in a science classroom. It is only to say that these texts may be of limited use in helping students learn how to use, create, and critique the texts central to the discipline and, thus, may hinder adolescents' learning of the content and process skills central to the discipline.

Another implication of our expanded definition of literacy is that content instruction cannot be separated from literacy instruction. One of the ways we determine whether our content instruction has been successful, or that students have learned, is by examining the ways in which they negotiate and create texts. For example, Ms. Baker, the mathematics teacher, ultimately will expect her students to create texts, perhaps in the form of equations, graphs, or explanations, in which they can demonstrate their understanding of linear equations. She may believe, like some mathematics teachers, that if the students understand the mathematical concepts, then making meaning and creating the texts used to represent those concepts will not present problems for the students. However, without sufficient literacy instruction, Ms.

Baker's students may struggle to create mathematically appropriate texts. In the case of mathematical explanations, Ms. Baker may expect her students to include justifications rather than simple descriptions—a distinction she may believe comes with deeper understanding of content. Ms. Baker may not realize that to ensure her students acquire this important mathematics literacy, she must engage in overt literacy instruction. Furthermore, this literacy instruction has the potential to strengthen students' conceptual understanding. Indeed, Ms. Baker's students, like all students, need to understand the content and how texts work within the discipline in order to be deemed knowledgeable and able within the discipline.

We have discussed three implications for our expanded definition of literacy: what counts as text is determined by the discipline, literacy instruction in content-area classrooms must focus on the texts and literacies central to the discipline, and content-area instruction cannot be separated from literacy instruction. These implications may challenge the roles traditionally taken by content-area teachers and literacy educators or specialists.

REDEFINING THE ROLES OF
CONTENT-AREA TEACHERS AND LITERACY SPECIALISTS

As we've already discussed, conflicts between content-area teachers and literacy specialists have arisen because content-area teachers do not perceive that their responsibility is to teach adolescents how to read and write (where reading and writing are defined narrowly as activities associated with traditional print texts), and literacy specialists, in an effort to encourage all teachers to address the literacy needs of adolescent students, recommend texts and literacies that may be only tangentially related to the activities associated with various disciplines. However, our expanded definitions of texts, literacy, reading, and writing can alleviate these tensions.

Under these broad definitions of texts and literacies, the responsibility to teach adolescents how to read and write discipline-specific texts falls squarely on the shoulders of content-area teachers. Content-area teachers must shoulder this responsibility for two reasons. First, the definition of literacy we present here suggests that being fully educated within a given discipline requires a level of sophistication and knowledge of the texts used to reason, communicate, and participate within that discipline. Thus, content-area literacy or discipline-specific literacy can be viewed as simply an aim of content learning. The second reason content-area teachers must take responsibility for teaching adolescents how to be literate in the discipline is that content-area teachers are knowledgeable about the texts and literacies central to the discipline. Indeed, we could not expect language arts teachers to understand the differences between how to frame and support historical and scientific arguments, much less how to write a mathematical proof or critique of a painting. Rather, content-area teachers must support the development of the discipline-specific literacies of the adolescents in their classrooms.

However, content-area teachers need not abandon the teaching of content in order to address literacy in their classrooms. Nor should they feel the need to introduce many new texts to their teaching as long as their instruction meets the national standards for content-area instruction in their particular disciplines. Instead, content-area teachers should identify the texts that naturally occur in their classrooms as a part of content instruction—both in terms of what adolescents must negotiate to develop their own understandings of content and what students must create to communicate those understandings. Returning to the vignette, Ms. Baker need not feel compelled to introduce texts beyond those associated with the mathematics she is teaching. Instead, she must become conscious of those texts and consider ways in which she can help her students improve their ability to interact with those texts.

Like other content-area teachers, Ms. Baker may need help to create instruction that enables her students to learn content and acquire the literacies associated with learning and doing mathematics. To this end, Ms. Santana, the literacy specialist, can be of assistance, despite her lack of experience with the discipline of mathematics. First, she could help Ms. Baker identify the various texts used to reason about, learn, and communicate mathematics. Then Ms. Santana could help Ms. Baker design lessons that would allow her to reveal her thinking while interacting with mathematics texts. "When you read the graph of a linear equation, what do you think about in order to make sense of the graph or the equation?" might be a useful question that Ms.

Santana could ask Ms. Baker. Once Ms. Baker reveals her thinking to Ms. Santana, they can work together to develop lessons that allow adolescents to learn how to engage in similar thinking practices as they interact with mathematics texts.

Note that the collaboration between Ms. Santana and Ms. Baker does not include Ms. Santana suggesting texts that are not central to learning, doing, or communicating mathematics (e.g., rap songs, poems, novels). Nor does it require Ms. Baker to abandon her teaching of linear equations. Instead, the collaboration focuses on important mathematical texts and the meaning-making activities associated with those texts—texts that are already part of Ms. Baker's mathematics instruction. In this way, both Ms. Baker and Ms. Santana offer particular expertise for their collaboration—Ms. Baker brings her expertise of mathematics, which includes her ability to meaningfully interact with mathematics texts, and Ms. Santana brings her expertise of literacy and her ability to focus instruction on texts and practices that support literacy learning and acquisition. However, both Ms. Baker and Ms. Santana also must acknowledge the limitations of their knowledge and, thus, the need to collaborate.

CHAPTER SUMMARY

We embrace literacy instruction that truly supports the acquisition and learning of content-area knowledge and that allows individuals to participate fully in disciplinary practices—this is at the heart of what we mean when we encourage literacy instruction across the curriculum. However, we don't universally accept *any* text or *any* literacy for *any* content-area classroom. Instead, we argue for *particular* texts and *particular* literacies for *particular* content-area classrooms. Certainly, disciplines like literature and history rely heavily on traditional print texts. Other disciplines, like visual arts and music education, rely more heavily on nontraditional, nonprint texts. Despite these particularities, all disciplines use a variety of traditional print and nontraditional, nonprint texts, as represented in Figure 2.1. Unfortunately, the limitations of the print text we have created here do not allow the diagonal line to be in motion. Instead, the reader must imagine that the diagonal line in the figure is in flux, thus representing the fact that the texts

FIGURE 2.1. The Proportion of Traditional and Non-Traditional Texts That Make Up Various Disciplines

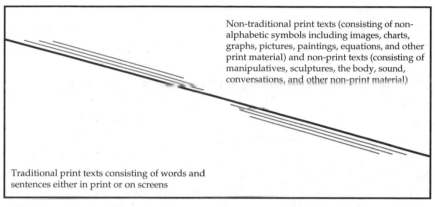

Non-traditional print texts (consisting of non-alphabetic symbols including images, charts, graphs, pictures, paintings, equations, and other print material) and non-print texts (consisting of manipulatives, sculptures, the body, sound, conversations, and other non-print material)

Traditional print texts consisting of words and sentences either in print or on screens

English   History   Science   Engineering   Mathematics   Theatre   Visual Arts   Music

central to the various disciplines change as the discipline changes. This figure demonstrates the need to attend to all literacies in content-area classrooms—both the print and the nonprint.

We acknowledge that the texts, literacies, and appropriate literacy instruction have not been identified for all content-area classrooms. And there is not a place where, say, a chemistry teacher can go to find literacy instructional ideas for teaching students how to meaningfully negotiate and create the texts associated with molecular modeling, balancing chemical equations, or acids and bases. Instead, the responsibility is on chemistry teachers to develop that literacy instruction—something they likely have little knowledge of how to do. Moreover, chemistry instruction that helps students gain facility with the texts and content central to learning and doing chemistry is vital to enabling students to be more chemistry-literate. Therefore, collaboration between content-area teachers and literacy specialists is crucial. Indeed, we maintain hope that (re)imagining literacy instruction for content-area classrooms can take place when content-area teachers and literacy specialists (re)imagine what counts as texts and literacies and work together to (re)imagine the instruction around those texts and literacies. This book is just a starting point.

Authors' note: The authors contributed equally to the preparation of this chapter.

REFERENCES

Ackerman, J. M. (1993). The promise of writing to learn. *Written Communication, 10,* 334–370.

Alvermann, D. E., & Moore, D. W. (1991). Secondary school reading. In R. Barr, M. L. Kamil, P. B. Mosenthal, & P. D. Pearson (Eds.), *Handbook of reading research* (Vol. 2, pp. 951–983). New York: Longman.

Bangert-Downs, R. L., Hurley, M. M., & Wilkinson, B. (2004). The effects of school-based writing-to-learn interventions on academic achievement: A meta-analysis. *Review of Educational Research, 74*(1), 29–58.

Bean, T. W. (2000). Reading in the content areas: Social constructivist dimensions. In M. L. Kamil, P. B. Mosenthal, P. D. Pearson, & R. Barr (Eds.), *Handbook of reading research* (Vol. 3, pp. 629–654). Mahwah, NJ: Erlbaum.

Bean, T. W., Bean, S. K., & Bean, K. F. (2001). Intergenerational conversations and two adolescents' multiple literacies: Implications for redefining content area literacy. In J. A. Rycik & J. L. Irvin (Eds.), *What adolescents deserve: A commitment to students' literacy learning* (pp. 207–225). Newark, DE: International Reading Association.

Bentley, D. (2008). *The icky sticky frog.* Atlanta, GA: Piggy Toes Press.

Conley, M. (2008). Cognitive strategy instruction for adolescents: What we know about the promise, what we don't know about the potential. *Harvard Educational Review, 78*(1), 84–106.

Cope, B., & Kalantzis, M. (Eds.). (2000). *Multiliteracies: Literacy learning and the design of social futures.* New York: Routledge.

Draper, R. J., & Siebert, D. (2004). Different goals, similar practices: Making sense of the mathematics and literacy instruction in a standards-based mathematics classroom. *American Educational Research Journal, 41*(4), 927–962.

Fisher, D., & Ivey, G. (2005). Literacy and language as learning in content-area classes: A departure from "every teacher a teacher of reading." *Action in Teacher Education, 277*(2), 3–11.

Gee, J. P. (2001). Reading as situated language: A sociocognitive perspective. *Journal of Adolescent and Adult Literacy, 44*(8), 714–725.

Gray, W. S. (1925). A modern program of reading instruction for the grades and high school. In G. M. Whipple (Ed.), *Report of the National Committee on Reading: 24th yearbook of the National Society for the Study of Education, Part 1* (pp. 21–73). Bloomington, IL: Public School Publishing Company.

McKenna, M. C., & Robinson, R. D. (1990). Content literacy: A definition and implications. *Journal of Reading, 34*(3), 184–186.

Moje, E. B., Overby, M., Tysvaer, N., & Morris, K. (2008). The complex world of adolescent literacy: Myths, motivations, and mysteries. *Harvard Educational Review, 78*(1), 107–154.

National Research Council. (1996). *National science education standards.* Washington, DC: National Academy Press.

National Research Council. (2000). *Inquiry and the national science education standards.* Washington, DC: National Academy Press.

Norris, S. P., & Phillips, L. M. (2003). How literacy in its fundamental sense is central to scientific literacy. *Science Education, 87*(2), 224–240.

Ruddell, M. R. (2005). *Teaching content reading and writing* (4th ed.). New York: Wiley.

Siebert, D., & Draper, R. J. (2008). Why content-area literacy messages do not speak to mathematics teachers: A critical content analysis. *Literacy Research and Instruction, 47*, 229–245.

Stewart, R. A., & O'Brien, D. G. (1989). Resistance to content area reading: A focus on preservice teachers. *Journal of Reading, 33*, 396–401.

Vacca, R. T. (2002). Making a difference in adolescents' school lives: Visible and invisible aspects of content area reading. In A. E. Farstrup & S. J. Samuels (Eds.), *What research has to say about reading instruction* (3rd ed., pp. 184–204). Newark, DE: International Reading Association.

CHAPTER 3

(Re)Imagining Literacies
for Mathematics Classrooms

Daniel Siebert
Scott Hendrickson

Current reform efforts in mathematics education are focused on helping students develop powerful understandings of mathematical concepts, procedures, and facts (National Council of Teachers of Mathematics [NCTM], 2000). It is no longer considered sufficient for mathematics instruction to focus merely on turning children into fast human calculators. In today's society, technology has largely removed the need for quick human computation. Instead, students need to be able to reason about quantitative situations, solve problems, form and test conjectures, communicate and evaluate mathematical reasoning, and model real-life contexts (National Research Council, 2001). Although some computational fluency is needed to be able to engage in these authentic mathematical activities, successful participants also will need a deep understanding of mathematics.

This emphasis on authentic mathematical activity and sense-making is reflected in new visions for mathematics instruction in the classroom (Martin, 2007). Instead of lessons that consist of the teacher demonstrating a new procedure and then assigning 30 exercises for students to complete so they can practice the procedure, recommendations from the national standards (NCTM, 2000) describe a student-centered, inquiry-based approach to instruction. In this type of instruction, students work together on tasks that engage them in developing important mathematical ideas, results, and procedures. The mathematics that emerges during these explorations is further illuminated through small-group and whole-class discussions. Rather than acting as the dispenser of knowledge and the arbiter of truth, the teacher takes on the role of facilitator in helping students discuss and make sense of their mathematical activity.

As suggested by Draper (2002), this emphasis on sense-making and understanding in the current mathematics education reform movement offers an excellent opportunity for literacy specialists to make an important contribution to the field of mathematics education. Students cannot engage in authentic mathematical activities unless they are able to read and write the many different types of texts that are used in these activities. Such texts include, but are not limited to, equations, graphs, diagrams, proofs, justifications, displays of manipulatives (e.g., base ten blocks), calculator readouts, verbal mathematical discussions, and written descriptions of problems. For each one of these types of texts, there is a specific literacy—a discipline-appropriate way of creating and interpreting a mathematical text—that students need to develop. Literacy specialists who can help mathematics teachers address these literacies in their teaching are poised to help both reform-oriented and traditional mathematics teachers increase the sense-making activity of their students.

PRINCIPLES FOR
LITERACY INSTRUCTION IN MATHEMATICS

Although there is potential for fertile relationships between literacy and mathematics educators, literacy educators should be cautious in making recommendations as they interact with mathematics teachers. Siebert and Draper (2008) found that many messages about content-area literacy that are directed at content-area teachers in general, and mathematics teachers specifically, are not appealing to mathematics educators. In particular, they found that these messages tended to overlook discipline-specific literacies and texts, minimize differences between disciplines, and misrepresent the discipline of mathematics. Messages that do not reference specific mathematical texts and literacies are problematic for mathematics teachers, because it is often unclear how these messages should be applied to the teaching and learning of mathematics. Messages that minimize the differences between disciplines or misrepresent mathematics are even more problematic, because they tend to lead to recommendations that directly violate mathematical norms and practices. Poor recommendations can damage the reputation of literacy educators and cause mathematics teachers to become even more resistant to literacy messages in the future. Even worse, these recommendations, if followed, can lead mathematics teachers to enact and teach incorrect mathematical practices and norms, doing students more harm than good.

To avoid crafting problematic literacy messages, literacy specialists might consider the following three principles for literacy instruction in the mathematics classroom:

> *Meaning Principle:* Mathematics instruction should emphasize
>   sense-making and understanding (Martin, 2007).
> *Activity Principle:* Mathematics instruction should engage students
>   in authentic mathematical activity.
> *Literacy Principle:* Literacy instruction should help students
>   become fluent with the texts they are using to make sense
>   of and engage in the mathematical activity.

These principles are described in more detail below.

The *Meaning Principle* states that mathematics instruction should focus on constructing meaning, building connections, and developing understanding. All mathematics, regardless of how abstract or symbol intensive, can be taught with meaning. Sometimes these meanings are built on previously learned abstract mathematics rather than real-world phenomena or experiences. Nevertheless, helping students uncover and understand these meanings is essential if students are to do more than just memorize definitions and procedures. Literacy messages that recognize the inherent meanings in the mathematics being taught are much more likely to be valued by mathematics teachers and lead to literacy instruction that enhances students' learning in mathematics. Literacy educators should never make recommendations that overlook or diminish mathematical meaning and understanding, such as recommending that children be taught to translate key words and numbers in story problems directly into equations (Manzo, Manzo, & Estes, 2001). Instead, messages and recommendations should support the development of meaning and understanding in the mathematics classroom.

The *Activity Principle* states that mathematics instruction should encourage and support authentic mathematical activity. As mentioned before, these activities include, but are not limited to, reasoning about quantitative situations, bounding and solving problems, forming and testing conjectures, communicating and evaluating mathematical reasoning, and modeling real-life contexts. These authentic mathematical activities are important for two reasons. First, they often embody the processes and provide the experiences necessary for students to come to understand important mathematical concepts, procedures, and facts. Second, developing the ability to engage in these activities is an essential part of coming to know mathematics, making it a legitimate end goal of mathematics instruction in and of itself. Rather than supplant authentic mathematical activity, such as having students study and write reports on famous mathematicians, literacy instruction in the mathematics classroom should be embedded within and enhance the ongoing authentic mathematical activity.

The *Literacy Principle* states that literacy instruction should help students develop fluency with the texts and literacies that currently are being used in mathematics classrooms rather than introduce new texts and literacies. Because all learning activities in mathematics involve texts that must be written and read in appropriate ways, there are mathematical texts and literacies that need to be addressed in every lesson. As mentioned earlier, these texts can range from equations to verbal discussions. The textbook itself can be considered a hybrid text composed of many different types of mathematical texts that must be read and coordinated with one another. Because literacy specialists may not be familiar with the types of texts that are common in mathematics classrooms, they may be tempted to introduce text types that are more familiar to them, such as written essays, poems, raps, or stories. Although these texts may have some pedagogical benefits, they nonetheless have limited use in mathematics because they are not well adapted for the purposes of communicating mathematics or engaging in authentic mathematical activity. Furthermore, focusing on the creation and use of texts that are seldom used to learn and do mathematics does not help students become proficient with the texts and literacies they need in order to gain access to mathematical ideas and practices.

EXAMPLES OF LITERACY INSTRUCTION IN MATHEMATICS

To illustrate how these principles might guide literacy instruction in a mathematics class, we present two vignettes. The first demonstrates how a general literacy instructional strategy can be modified to address students' literacy needs as they engage in problem solving. The second presents a teacher-led discussion that guides students in learning to read and make sense of equations in terms of the real-world context the equations are meant to model. Following each vignette is a discussion of how the meaning, activity, and literacy principles were incorporated into the mathematics lesson.

Vignette 1: After attending a literacy workshop, a group of secondary mathematics teachers decide to modify the K-W-L (Ogle, 1986) instructional reading strategy (K—What do I know? W—What do I want to know? L—What did I learn by completing the reading?) to make it more appropriate for the mathematics classroom. They rename the strategy K-W-S to fit questions framed to support students' reasoning and problem-solving strategies (K—What do I know about the problem situation based on given information or prior experience? W—What do I want or need to know in order to answer the questions stated in the problem? S—What strategies might I use to answer the questions?). One of the teachers, Ms. Hall, volunteers to try the strategy out in her precalculus class with the following problem:

In the Lead

Our favorite track star, Speedy, has a friend named Sporty who is also quite athletic. Although running isn't always Sporty's best event, the two friends like to race against each other.

You will recall that a sports analyst recently studied a film of a race in which Speedy competed. The analyst came up with the formula $m(t) = 0.1t^2 + 3t$ to describe the distance Speedy had run t seconds after beginning the race. The same analyst came up with the expression $n(t) = 0.095t^2 + 2.92t$ to describe how far Sporty has run t seconds after the start of the race.

If the two friends follow these racing strategies, how far ahead will the winner be in a 400-meter race? (Fendel, Resek, Alper, & Fraser, 2000)

As students fill out the K-W-S chart, Ms. Hall observes them noting things that were not explicitly stated in the text. For example, many students write the questions, "Who wins the race?" and "How long does it take for each runner to cross the finish line?" in the W-column. Some students make and record an inference, "Speedy is always ahead of Sporty," in the K-column, based on their understanding of the magnitude of the numbers and the meaning of the operations used in the formulas that give the positions of the two runners after the start of the race (see Figure 3.1). She realizes that this instructional tool has provided access to the mathematics of this problem for many students who previously have struggled with situated contexts.

FIGURE 3.1. A Sample K-W-S Table for the Story Problem "In the Lead"

K	W	S
What do I *know*?	What do I *want* or *need* to know?	What *strategies* might I use?
Formula for Speedy's distance as a function of time	How far ahead is the winner at the end of the race?	Make tables showing the distance run by each racer after different amounts of elapsed time.
Formula for Sporty's distance as a function of time	Who wins the race?	
	How long does it take for the winner to cross the finish line?	Sketch graphs of distance as a function of time.
They are running a 400-meter race		
Speedy is always ahead of Sporty		Create the function $m(t) - n(t)$
		Solve $m(t) = 400$

In this first vignette, Ms. Hall introduces a modified K-W-L literacy strategy to help her students develop *meaning* for a story problem by identifying important quantities, the relationships between these quantities, and the strategies that can be used to find the values of the important quantities whose values are unknown. Based on past experience, Ms. Hall knows that her students do not have difficulty with decoding a story problem, understanding the context of a foot race, or attributing meaning to quadratic equations. Instead, they struggle with identifying quantities and reasoning about the relationships between quantities in the story context. The modified K-W-L is particularly well suited for helping students recognize quantities that might be important in this particular context, even quantities that are not named in the problem. The modification to identify strategies helps students reason about what operations can be performed on known quantities to yield the value of pertinent unknown quantities.

The K-W-S strategy used in this vignette directly supports, not displaces, the authentic mathematical *activity* of problem solving in two important ways. First, the strategy scaffolds students' efforts to identify and describe relationships between quantities, an important aspect of problem solving. Second, the K-W-S strategy supports the students' attempts to tackle a problem situation that they do not have a ready-made procedure for solving. One of the key characteristics of authentic problem solving is that students do not have a pre-existing solution method or procedure available to them to solve the problem. The K-W-S format prompts students to develop and record possible strategies for solving the problem.

The K-W-S strategy was used to assist students in developing *literacy* by helping them read and understand, in mathematically powerful ways, a text that was already part of a lesson. Students often encounter word problems in mathematics lessons. These story problems can range anywhere from the highly stylized problems in traditional curricula (e.g., "A train travels west at 90 km/hr as a second train travels north at 110 km/hr . . .") to the longer, more involved story problems from reform-oriented curricula, like the story problem above. The K-W-S strategy promotes a discipline-appropriate reading of the story problem, identifying three particular types of questions that expert problem solvers often ask as they read and solve story problems. As students consider and answer these questions, they have the opportunity to learn and practice a discipline-appropriate way of reading and solving a story problem.

Vignette 2: Students in an algebra 1 class are asked to develop a formula to figure out how many one-foot square border tiles would be needed to surround an in-ground, square hot tub that is s (an unknown number of) feet on each side. As students work on this task, they generate different expressions depending on how they visualize counting the tiles. The next day the teacher presents a compilation of these expressions as "texts" and asks the other students to "read" the expressions and determine how the original authors had thought about the counting task. For example, students decide that someone who wrote $4s + 4$ saw s tiles along each of the four sides plus the four corner tiles, while someone who wrote $4(s + 1)$ saw the tiles arranged in four groups of size $s + 1$ on each side (see Figure 3.2). Students were surprised at the number of different expressions that could be written to count the number of

FIGURE 3.2. Examples of Students' Algebraic Expressions That Reflect Their Ways of Counting Border Tiles Around a Square Hot Tub

Symbolic Expression	Visual Interpretation
Write an expression to represent the number of one-foot square border tiles surrounding an in-ground square hot tub that is s feet on each side.	
$N = 4s + 4$	
$N = 4(s + 1)$	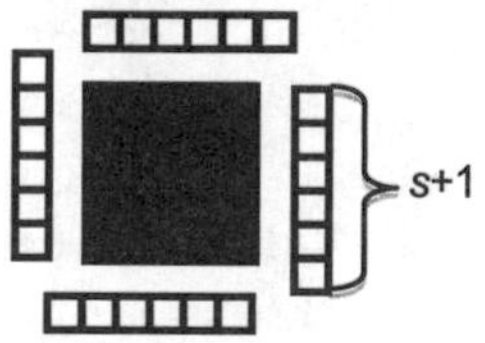
$N = 2s + 2(s + 2)$	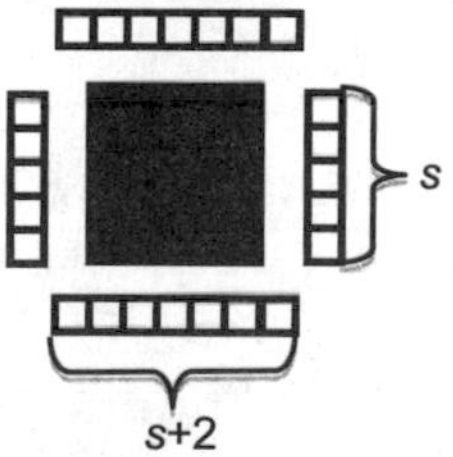
$N = 4(s + 2) - 4$	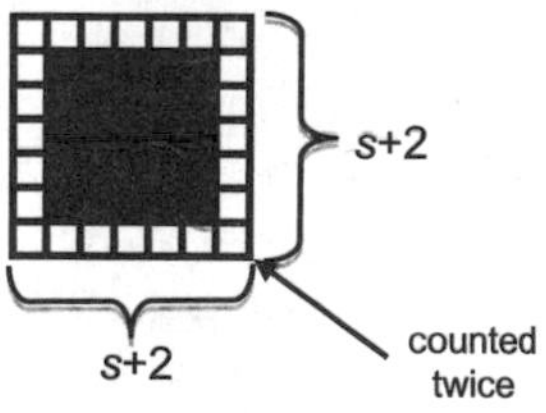
$N = (s + 2)^2 - s^2$	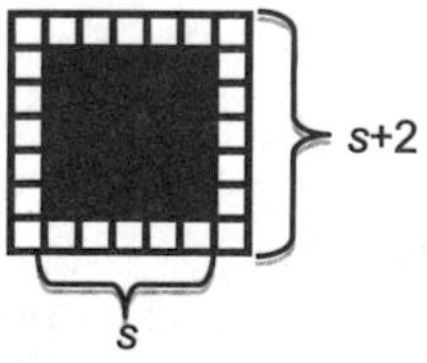

border tiles. They also were surprised that they could figure out what another student was thinking just from the written notation. They realized that in this situation the symbolic notation could be used to "tell a story."

As the lesson progressed, one student asked, "Isn't 4(s + 1) the same as 4s + 4?" Seizing the opportunity to allow her students to engage with the symbolic notation of algebra, the teacher asked this student to explain his thinking. "It's like the distributive property, four groups of size s + 1 is the same as four groups of size s plus 4 groups of size 1."

The teacher was pleased that this student could visualize the distributive property in the two different arrangements of the tiles. She encouraged other students to find ways to demonstrate the equivalence of the other expressions they had written to the simpler expression 4s + 4. As students carried out various symbolic manipulations, such as using the distributive property or combining like terms, they illustrated the result of the manipulation by rearranging the tiles into new groupings that matched their symbols.

In this vignette, students are asked to write *meaningful* algebraic expressions that model the tile situation and to develop *meaning* for the algebraic expressions of other students. To do this, students engage in counting tiles around the perimeter of tubs of various sizes until they find a pattern and can represent that pattern as an algebraic expression. Sense-making serves as an important guideline for reading and writing these expressions, since in this classroom it is expected that students will be able to justify why their expressions are viable models of the situation. The teacher's decision to engage students in the literacy activity of publishing their algebraic expressions and reading the algebraic expressions of others leads to increased understanding in the students as they see how various algebraic expressions capture different patterns in the perimeter.

Students also are engaged in authentic mathematical *activities*, namely, creating a model of a real-world context and understanding the models created by others. An integral part of creating and evaluating models of real-world phenomena is the ability to perceive parts of the mathematical model as representing certain aspects of the real-world context. In this situation, students come to see s, s + 1, and s + 2 as representing different lengths, measured in tiles, along the edges of the hot tub. Not only does the literacy activity of publishing and reading algebraic expressions enable the authentic mathematical activity of modeling real-world contexts, but it is an absolutely necessary part of the activity itself. Thus, the literacy activity that the students are engaged in supports and enables the ongoing authentic mathematical activity.

The literacy activity of publishing and reading algebraic expressions helps students develop *literacy* skills by focusing on reading and coordinating two types of texts that are already embedded in the lesson: the diagram of the hot tub and the algebraic expressions themselves. Rearranging the tiles to match the symbolic manipulations being carried out by various students allows them to use one representational system, the tiles, to gain deeper insight into another representational system, the symbols and properties of algebra. As the students "read" each of the expressions and draw pictures to represent what the authors who created these expressions might have been thinking, they recognize that each expression tells a different yet equivalent story, and that these expressions are not just symbols to manipulate, but also stories to be interpreted. Students learn to manipulate the diagram of the hot tub in different ways so as to see parts of the algebraic expressions in the diagram, as demonstrated in Figure 3.2. This method of coordinating diagrams and algebraic expressions is an important literate act in the discipline of mathematics.

ARGUING FOR THE IMPORTANCE OF LITERACY INSTRUCTION IN MATHEMATICS CLASSROOMS

What we have tried to illustrate is how literacy instruction that follows the three principles can fit well with mathematics teaching that is focused on meaning-making and authentic mathematical activity. Our intention to this point has been to provide insights into the discipline of mathematics, insights that can help literacy specialists understand what mathematics teachers may believe and value. We anticipate that this knowledge can enable literacy educators to craft literacy messages and recommendations that are more relevant to and more easily accepted by mathematics teachers than literacy messages of the past.

At the same time, we also recognize that even if literacy messages and recommendations adhere to the above principles, mathematics teachers may still be unwilling to listen unless they understand the essential role that literacy plays in mathematics teaching and learning. To help literacy specialists further persuade mathematics teachers to consider implementing literacy instruction into their daily mathematics teaching, we present the following argument, which we as mathematics teachers personally find persuasive and motivating. This argument consists of (a) noting that successful mathematics learning requires literacy instruction in the texts and literacies of mathematics, (b) arguing that literacy instruction can fit seamlessly into everyday mathematics lessons, and (c) acknowledging the mathematics teacher as the most qualified person to teach this type of literacy.

If the notion of texts is broadened to include everything that people imbue with meaning, then clearly literacy is an issue that must be addressed in every mathematics lesson. Because meaning cannot be transferred directly from mind to mind, every lesson involves some type of text that must be created and used in particular ways in order for meanings to be conveyed, negotiated, and understood. Thus, mathematics learning cannot be separated from the texts students are creating and using to learn mathematics. Stated another way, when students struggle, teachers cannot dismiss the possibility that the problem may be a lack of fluency with mathematical texts rather than a misunderstanding of mathematical ideas or procedures. Teachers who want their students to learn mathematics must address not only mathematical content, but also the texts that are being used to create, convey, and negotiate that content.

Mathematics teachers may worry that they do not have time to include literacy instruction. However, the above principles for literacy instruction in mathematics can serve as guidelines to help mathematics teachers create literacy instruction that fits seamlessly into their mathematics lessons and supports their mathematics instructional goals. The first two principles ensure that the literacy instruction supports the meaning-making and mathematical activity that is central to the lesson. The third principle guides mathematics teachers to search for the texts that students are creating and using during the lesson, to consider what students need to know about how these texts should be created and used, and then to design instruction that helps students develop fluency with these texts. As mathematics teachers adopt a literacy lens through which to view their mathematics instruction, they are likely to discover that they are already helping their students learn how to create and use some of the mathematical texts that occur in their classrooms. By noticing all of the texts and literacies needed to learn and do mathematics and following the three principles above, mathematics teachers are positioned to design even better literacy instruction than what they are already providing.

It is important that mathematics teachers recognize that they are uniquely qualified and ultimately responsible for teaching literacy in mathematics. Mathematics teachers are likely to be among the few teachers in their schools who know how to read and write mathematical texts in discipline-appropriate ways. Because of this knowledge, they are better prepared than anyone else to help students become literate with these texts. Furthermore, because students will encounter the literacies essential to doing mathematics most often in their mathematics classes, mathematics teachers must teach these literacies or students will not develop them. But perhaps most important of all, the ability to create and use mathematics texts in appropriate ways is part of what counts as knowing mathematics. Mathematics teachers must help their students develop these literacies if they wish to claim that they are truly teaching mathematics.

COLLABORATION AS A STARTING POINT

We anticipate that although the principles of *meaning*, *activity*, and *literacy* can be helpful to both literacy specialists and mathematics teachers, the principles by themselves do not provide enough direction for either literacy specialists or mathematics teachers as they first begin to design literacy instruction in mathematics. Literacy specialists are likely to lack knowledge about what mathematical meanings are possible and preferable during a mathematics lesson, what characteristics an activity must have in order to qualify as a particular type of authentic mathematical activity, which objects in a lesson are to be used as texts, and how those objects should be written and read. In contrast, mathematics teachers are likely to have difficulty identifying texts and literacies in their teaching. Furthermore, once they have identified these texts and literacies, it is just as likely that they will have limited knowledge of how to craft literacy instruction to address them.

Together, literacy specialists and mathematics teachers possess the knowledge and skills to create literacy instruction that can help students develop fluency with mathematical texts. Literacy specialists can teach mathematics teachers what qualifies as texts and the essential role that literacy plays in learning mathematical content. Literacy specialists also have a wealth of knowledge about different literacy instructional strategies, such as K-W-L. Although they may not be able to identify a strategy that accomplishes the literacy goals of a particular lesson, they nonetheless may be able to suggest strategies that can be modified to suit the goals of the lesson, such as K-W-S in Vignette 1. On the other hand, mathematics teachers can identify the important meanings and understanding they want their students to develop. They can orchestrate instruction so that students are engaged in authentic activities. With prompting from the literacy educator, they can identify the objects that are treated as texts, which they will likely know how to read and write in discipline-appropriate ways, such as in Vignette 2. Taken together, the combined skill set of literacy specialists and mathematics teachers is exactly what is needed to develop literacy instruction for the mathematics classroom.

It is likely that collaborations between literacy specialists and mathematics teachers will have to be initiated by the literacy specialists, because mathematics teachers normally will not recognize that they and their students are working with texts. Once again, the three principles of *meaning*, *activity*, and *literacy* can help guide initial collaborations. For example, the literacy specialist can ask the mathematics teacher what the instructional goals of a lesson are, paying particularly close attention to descriptions of important mathematical meanings and understandings, and what authentic mathematical activities the students will be engaged in. Note that if the mathematics teacher tends to engage in traditional mathematics instruction, it is likely that he or she will talk more about the procedures or computations the students should master rather than about important mathematical meanings or authentic activities. In this case, the literacy specialist can ask questions to guide the teacher in considering what students must understand in order to know how, when, and why they perform the desired computations, as well as what types of activities might be used to help the students develop these understandings. Whether the teacher leans toward reform-oriented or traditional mathematics instruction, the literacy specialist can listen for clues about what objects (i.e., texts) are important for students to use and create as they engage in the lesson. By steering the discussion toward how to support students' developing fluency with these texts, the literacy specialist can help the mathematics teacher realize the need for literacy instruction, simultaneously pointing out how literacy instruction might support the mathematics teacher's goals for the lesson.

CHAPTER SUMMARY

In this chapter we have argued that mathematical literacy is important for supporting meaning-making and authentic mathematical activity. It is also a worthy end goal in and of itself. Literacy instruction that follows the three principles of *meaning*, *activity*, and *literacy* can help address both the literacy and mathematical needs of students. Although literacy specialists may lack the necessary knowledge about the discipline of mathematics to create literacy instruction that follows the three principles, they nonetheless can be catalysts for helping mathematics teachers meet students' literacy needs. As they do so, they have the opportunity to make important differences in the lives of adolescents and the mathematics teachers who teach them.

REFERENCES

Draper, R. J. (2002). School mathematics reform, constructivism, and literacy: A case for literacy instruction in reform-oriented mathematics classrooms. *Journal of Adolescent and Adult Literacy, 45,* 520–529.

Fendel, D., Resek, D., Alper, L., & Fraser, S. (2000). *Interactive mathematics program, year 4.* Emeryville, CA: Key Curriculum Press.

Manzo, A. V., Manzo, U. C., & Estes, T. H. (2001). *Content area literacy: Interactive teaching for active learning* (3rd ed.). New York: Wiley.

Martin, T. S. (Ed.). (2007). *Mathematics teaching today* (2nd ed.). Reston, VA: National Council of Teachers of Mathematics.

National Council of Teachers of Mathematics. (2000). *Principles and standards for school mathematics.* Reston, VA: Author.

National Research Council. (2001). *Adding it up: Helping children learn mathematics.* Washington, DC: National Academy Press.

Ogle, D. (1986). K-W-L: A teaching model that develops active reading of expository text. *The Reading Teacher, 39,* 564–570.

Siebert, D., & Draper, R. J. (2008). Why content-area literacy messages do not speak to mathematics teachers: A critical content analysis. *Literacy Research and Instruction, 47,* 229–245.

CHAPTER 4

(Re)Imagining Literacies for History Classrooms

Jeffery D. Nokes

Students in Ms. Robinson's 8th-grade American history class explore the concept of culture while learning about the way archeologists study the past. Ms. Robinson teaches students about archeologists' work—the way they use artifacts, make observations, and make inferences based on those observations and on their own prior research. She introduces the challenges presented in studying prehistoric people who left behind no written records. To prepare the students for an activity, she shows some broken shards of pottery and asks students to help her make observations. She observes out loud that all of the pieces except one are the same two colors, tan and reddish. The other piece is lighter. One student notices that many shards appear to fit together. She and the students continue to make observations. Then she asks the class to help her make inferences based on the observations. The class puts the pieces together and students visualize the size and shape of the pot they reconstruct. Camille points out that the odd-colored shard must be from a different pot since it doesn't match the other pieces. Students continue to make inferences about what the pot might have been used for and why a shard of pottery from another vessel might have been mixed in with the rest of the pieces.

After several minutes of analysis, the students are assigned to work in small groups analyzing other facsimiles of artifacts from the Ancestral Pueblo culture. Each student uses a record sheet to sketch the artifact and list observations and inferences. One group looks at a picture of a cliff dwelling. Ms. Robinson walks past the group, notices a lull in their conversation, and asks, "How many people do you think lived there? Is there something there in the picture that could help you make an inference about that?" The students agree that there were a lot of people living there. Jake quickly counts about 35 separate rooms in the cliff dwelling. Sarah asks whether each family had its own room. Candace suggests that the rooms look too small for a whole family. "Maybe each family had a couple of rooms," Jim responds. "Maybe each person had their own room," Sarah suggests. In other groups similar types of discussions occur about small pieces of hemp rope, stone arrowheads, a tanned rabbit skin, some cobs of hard-kernel corn, and other artifacts. After a few minutes Ms. Robinson asks groups to exchange artifacts, and conversations resume with the new evidence.

Across town, students in Mr. Ramos's 11th-grade U.S. history class study the Battle of New Orleans. Mr. Ramos wants them to construct an understanding of the battle from multiple texts from a variety of sources. He has collected a song, a letter, a painting, a journal entry, a map, and a textbook account of the battle. He has prepared a graphic organizer that has a place for students to write about the source of each text, including its author, audience, and purpose; summarize the content of the text; make direct comparisons between the various texts; and evaluate the accuracy of the text's content. He plays a recording of Johnny Horton's song "The Battle of New Orleans" (Driftwood, 1959) while students read the lyrics. At the end of the song he gives students the graphic organizer and he leads them in an analysis of the source of the song: "Who was Johnny Horton? Did he write the song or was he just the singer? Who was his intended audience? How did the author know about the events of the battle? When was the song written? What was its purpose?" Students then summarize the content of the song. Mr. Ramos asks, "Do you think that if you were there at the battle it would have looked like this song portrays it? Do you think that they actually put cannon balls in alligators' mouths and 'powdered their behinds'? Why would the writer write this if it weren't true?" Mr. Ramos leads a discussion as the students analyze and evaluate this song as a historical record. Students receive other texts in a packet and with a partner conduct a similar analysis of them, this time comparing and contrasting the content of each text. At the conclusion of the class Mr. Ramos leads a discussion on what students think really happened at the Battle of New Orleans, and which texts were most useful in helping them construct this understanding.

These two vignettes illustrate history classrooms where literacy is an important part of the curriculum—not literacy in a general sense but literacy specific to the discipline of history. In both situations, teachers help students create their own historical interpretations based on multiple, fragmentary, and sometimes contradictory resources. Teachers provide students with support to help them negotiate these texts. Students engage in reading, analyzing, and thinking in ways similar to methods used in historical inquiry by archeologists and historians. Both vignettes represent a break from traditional history instruction. Indeed, historical literacy instruction does not occur very often in secondary history classrooms (Nokes & Hansen, 2007).

Instead, history teachers rely heavily on textbooks (American Textbook Council, 1994–95; Paxton, 1999, U.S. Department of Education, 2006) and lecture (Nokes & Hansen, 2007) to teach historical content. Very often, during the majority of class time, students passively receive information by listening to a lecture or by looking in their textbook for answers to questions posed by the textbook authors or their teacher. Historical documents are rarely used and students are not taught to appreciate their value in historical inquiry. In classrooms where lectures and textbooks dominate instructional time, students develop a distorted perception of what it means to learn history. Historical thinking, in their view, involves remembering information until the next test. These classrooms do not give students any sense of the work of historians or what it means to engage in historical inquiry. It is not surprising that secondary students consistently rate history as one of the most boring, least favorite classes (Schug, 1982). This type of lecture and textbook instruction has been under attack since the late 1800s when Hall (1883) wrote, "The high educational value of history is too great to be left to teachers who . . . [keep their] finger on the place in the textbook and only [ask] questions conveniently printed for them in the margin or the back of the book" (p. v).

In recent years, a growing number of literacy advocates, history pedagogy experts, and secondary teachers have joined Hall (1883) in voicing a need to change history instruction (Britt & Aglinskas, 2002; Nokes, Dole, & Hacker, 2007; Wineburg, 1991, 1998). They conceive of classrooms where students learn not only about the past, but about the study of the past. They suggest that teachers teach not simply the content of history but the process of historical inquiry. They encourage teachers to teach not only the historical narrative but the methods used to write it (Stahl & Shanahan, 2004). In short, they suggest that teachers instruct students on the literacies of history. In a traditional class, a teacher might lecture on the home front during World War II and include a few multiple-choice questions about it on the unit test. On the other hand, in a classroom focused on historical literacy, students might interview several women and men who remember life during World War II, synthesize their stories into an article on the effects of the war on their neighborhood, and submit the article to a local newspaper for publication. Thus, in history classrooms where literacy instruction occurs, students are invited into the community of practice and learn how to negotiate and create the texts that are valued by historians. The national standards for history promote historical literacy instruction by urging teachers to teach students to engage in historical analysis. These standards acknowledge the unique methods, texts, and thinking of historians. For example, they recommend that secondary students be taught to identify the source of documents, differentiate between facts and interpretations, consider multiple perspectives, hold interpretations as tentative, interrogate historical data, and marshal evidence to support interpretations (Nash & Crabtree, 1996).

These standards reflect a growing body of research on the literacies associated with historical thinking. A brief review of this research will prepare literacy specialists to work appropriately with history teachers to address students' needs. Research has answered, or is in the process of answering, three questions on the teaching of historical literacies to students: (1) how do historians construct meaning with multiple texts, (2) how do students instinctively engage with historical texts, and (3) how can teachers help students read and think more like historians?

HOW DO HISTORIANS
CONSTRUCT MEANING WITH MULTIPLE TEXTS?

Wineburg (1991, 1998) pioneered research on historians' reading. He and other researchers found that historians are unusually active, skillful, and critical readers. They approach a reading task with healthy skepticism, recognizing that texts are evidence rather than repositories of facts (Britt & Aglinskas, 2002). As historians read, they recognize the tentative nature of historical understanding and are willing to change their perspectives in light of new evidence. They do not take information in texts at face value but use three heuristics to evaluate and analyze the content of historical texts: sourcing, corroboration, and contextualization (Wineburg, 1991). *Sourcing* is the use of a text's source to comprehend and evaluate its content (Wineburg, 1991). Historians view all documents as interpretations of events through emotional, biased, imperfect witnesses. They understand that texts can be fully understood and evaluated only when the source is acknowledged. *Corroboration* entails making connections between information found in different texts, with contradictions and similarities being noted (Britt & Aglinskas, 2002; Wineburg, 1991). Before accepting information found in one text as plausible, historians check it against the content of other texts. *Contextualization* is an effort to comprehend and evaluate documents with the geographic, political, historical, and cultural context of their creation in mind (Wineburg, 1991). These three heuristics—sourcing, corroboration, and contextualization—are used universally by historians and form the foundation of historical literacy.

Historians make a distinction among primary sources, texts that give a firsthand, eyewitness account of an event, such as a journal, pencil sketch, or letter; secondary sources, texts that are created by an outsider using primary sources, such as a historian's essay, a bar graph, or a newspaper account; and tertiary sources, texts that are written using secondary sources, such as textbooks, a webpage, or encyclopedia articles. Historians value primary sources above secondary and tertiary sources for obvious reasons—primary sources give an account of an event with a single layer of bias. Historians' interpretations add a second layer of bias to secondary sources. Much of the work of historians involves trying to sift through these layers of bias to gain an accurate understanding of past events. Thus, for students, the ability to distinguish among primary, secondary, and tertiary sources is an important element of historical literacy.

Although traditional print texts form a foundation of historical study, nonprint texts are also useful. Prehistoric cultures, which left no written records, are studied by the artifacts that they left behind. Meaning is negotiated with these artifacts in particular ways that form the foundation of archeology. For example, two of the strategies used by archeologists are observation-making and inference-making. In addition to archeologists using artifacts, historians study historic cultures, trends, and events using artifacts to supplement written evidence. The tools, art, music, weaponry, and architecture of a society reveal much to those who are astute at making observations and appropriate inferences. Further, political cartoons, maps, sketches, photographs, speeches, radio programs, television programs, movies, and clothing styles also can indicate the values and attributes of different peoples. These texts, and numerous others, are all negotiated by historians as they develop an understanding of the past.

In addition to negotiating various texts, historians also create an assortment of texts to help others understand their theories about the past. For example, historians create monographs, maps, cartograms, population pyramids, charts, graphs, and diagrams that illustrate historical trends or concepts. In order to enter the community of practice, students must be able to negotiate meaning with both the texts studied and the texts created by historians. Using the model of historians, students who are historically literate should be able to (a) create historical interpretations using a wide variety of print and nonprint texts; (b) distinguish among primary, secondary, and tertiary sources; (c) use historians' literacy strategies, most notably, sourcing, corroboration, contextualization, observation-making, and inference-making; and (d) display the habits of mind associated with historical inquiry, such as recognizing the tentative nature of historical interpretations and possessing a healthy skepticism.

HOW DO STUDENTS
INSTINCTIVELY ENGAGE WITH HISTORICAL TEXTS?

Not surprisingly, research has shown that high school students do not instinctively negotiate texts the way historians do. Students tend to read print texts in linear fashion. They accept the contents of all texts at face value and make an effort to remember facts rather than understand an event. They become frustrated when multiple texts contradict one another (Wineburg, 1991). Students do not naturally engage in sourcing, corroboration, or contextualization, nor do they exhibit the habits of mind (i.e., viewing documents as evidence, maintaining an open mind, having a healthy skepticism) that historians possess (Wineburg, 1991). Britt and Aglinskas (2002) found that neither high school students nor undergraduate students effectively employed sourcing to critically evaluate texts, even when prompted to do so. In fact, both high school and college students referred to material from a novel as if it were factual, a tendency also observed by Wineburg (1991). Although not directly related to history, research has shown that students have similar challenges in thinking critically about information found on the Internet (Leu et al., 2007). In spite of these challenges, Stahl, Hynd, Britton, McNish, and Bosquet (1996) found that engagement with primary sources was productive for students, many of whom were able to remember the basic facts about an historical event after reading two related documents.

HOW CAN TEACHERS HELP STUDENTS
READ AND THINK MORE LIKE HISTORIANS?

Numerous studies have shown that students can learn to engage in more sophisticated analysis of multiple historical texts of a variety of genres. Studies have found that practice in analytical writing with feedback (Young & Leinhardt, 1998), explicit strategy instruction on historical methodology (Britt & Aglinskas, 2002; Ferretti, MacArthur, & Okolo, 2001; Nokes et al., 2007; VanSledright, 2002), and combinations of direct instruction on historiography and writing instruction (De La Paz, 2005) lead to the increased use of historians' strategies. A synthesis of these studies seems to indicate that in order to improve students' ability to analyze texts like historians, teachers must provide several opportunities for their students to interact with multiple texts of various types and must provide instruction on the literacies of history. Research on literacy suggests that effective literacy instruction often takes one of two forms: explicit strategy instruction or implicit strategy instruction. Literacy advocates recommend a mix of the two types of instruction (Dole, Duffy, Roehler, & Pearson, 1991; Vacca, 2002). The vignettes at the start of this chapter illustrate explicit and implicit historical literacy instruction, and each type is discussed below as it is applied in the vignettes.

LITERACY INSTRUCTION IN HISTORY CLASSES

In the first vignette, Ms. Robinson provides *explicit* instruction on the strategies used by archeologists to study artifacts. In the second vignette, Mr. Ramos provides *implicit* strategy instruction, leading students to use sourcing and corroboration as they study documents related to the Battle of New Orleans. An explanation of each of these instructional methods will be given as well as an analysis of each vignette.

Explicit Strategy Instruction

Explicit strategy instruction typically occurs in four stages. First, the teacher explains a literacy strategy to students. As part of this explanation the teacher names the strategy, discusses when it is useful, presents how the strategy is used, and explains why it works. Second, the teacher models the strategy by "thinking aloud" in order to reveal the thought processes used. Students can model the strategy for one another by describing their thought processes to their peers. Third, students practice the strategy with temporary support or "scaffolding." This support comes in a variety of formats, such as working with peers, working with particularly easy texts, receiving reminders about the process, or using teacher-prepared graphic organizers. Fourth, the teacher provides an opportunity for students to practice the strategy without support. A more detailed account of Ms. Robinson's class studying the Ancestral Pueblo illustrates the four stages of explicit strategy instruction.

Ms. Robinson teaches students the strategies of observation-making and inference-making, both important in historical inquiry, particularly in working with nonprint texts. During stage one she makes sure that students know what it means to make an observation. The class discusses the characteristics of an observant person. Ms. Robinson leads the class in a similar discussion on inference-making, explaining that good inferences are based on observations and background knowledge.

During the second stage Ms. Robinson models observation-making and inference-making for her students. Using shards of pottery, she explains that these are facsimiles of artifacts found at ancient Ancestral Pueblo sites and that she wants to see what the class can discover about the people who left them behind. She thinks aloud while the students listen. She notes that some of the edges of the pottery shards are smooth and some are rough, as if they had been broken. She notices the colors and the coldness of each piece. She invites the class to think aloud with her, and they add that one piece doesn't look like the others and that some of the pieces appear to fit together. Eventually she and the class piece them together. After modeling observation-making she begins to model inference-making. She muses,

"I wonder what this would be if we had all the pieces." She listens as the students make guesses and critique one another's guesses. She comments again, "I wonder what it might have been used for." And she listens as students offer guesses and critique one another's ideas. When one student says that he thinks it was a pot used for cooking, she asks, "Is there any other observation we would expect to make on a cooking pot?" Students look again and notice some burn marks on the side of some of the pieces. "Are there any alternative theories about why there might be burned, broken pottery?" she continues. "Maybe they were attacked and their village burned," Steve suggests. Students begin to debate alternative theories as Ms. Robinson moderates. When the conversation on the pottery shards begins to lag, Ms. Robinson moves from the modeling stage of the lesson to the guided practice stage.

During stage three, guided practice, Ms. Robinson asks students to get into cooperative-learning groups and she gives each student a study guide that they will use to keep a written record of their analysis of each artifact. The study guide provides support for their reading of the artifacts by having them keep a record of their work in three columns. In the first column students are asked to make a sketch of the artifact. In the second column they record important observations. In the third they record their inferences. At the bottom of the page they are asked to summarize their understanding of the culture of the Ancestral Pueblo people based on the evidence they have analyzed. Ms. Robinson gives each group a different artifact, and she moves around the room as they conduct their analyses. She pauses with some groups to ask a thought-provoking question, but mostly she allows them to develop and critique their own ideas. After a few minutes Ms. Robinson asks students to exchange artifacts and a new analysis begins. The majority of class time is spent in this way, with Ms. Robinson, the peer groups, and the study guide providing scaffolding.

With 10 minutes of class left, Ms. Robinson moves into the fourth stage, independent practice. She asks the class members to move to their original seats and, without help, write a few paragraphs about the way the Ancestral Pueblo lived. She reminds students that they, like historians, must cite evidence (i.e., observations) to support each inference that they write about. At the end of class, Ms. Robinson collects the papers and reads them to assess class members' understanding of the Ancestral Pueblo and their ability to make plausible inferences based on observations. She starts class the next day with a debriefing on the activity, a review of the work of archeologists, and a reminder about the strategies of observation-making and inference-making.

Implicit Strategy Instruction

Some history teachers may be more comfortable providing implicit rather than explicit strategy instruction. Unlike explicit strategy instruction, when providing implicit strategy instruction the teacher does not openly discuss the strategy with students. Instead, students are given an assignment that guides them into the use of a strategy. The strategy is not named or talked about. Nevertheless, in the process of completing the assignment, the strategy is practiced. The intent is that with repeated use of a strategy, students will incorporate it into their habits of thinking. Literacy researchers recommend a balance of explicit and implicit strategy instruction in content-area classrooms (Vacca, 2002). A more detailed account of Mr. Ramos's lesson on the Battle of New Orleans illustrates implicit strategy instruction.

Mr. Ramos has designed a lesson to give students practice in sourcing and corroboration, two heuristics historians use as they negotiate historical texts. He has created a study guide that prompts students to consider the source of each document. In order to increase the likelihood that students will pay attention to the source, he has selected a wide variety of texts, both primary and secondary sources, that represent different perspectives. He hopes the class will engage in a sophisticated level of sourcing—that they will not merely name the source but will explain the content of the text with the source in mind. He knows his students will respond well to the song "The Battle of New Orleans" (Driftwood, 1959) and that the class will be able to have a good discussion about how the author and performers had a particular purpose in creating and recording the song, and about how that purpose had a profound influence on the content of the song.

In addition, Mr. Ramos has chosen texts that contain contradictory and fragmentary information. To facilitate corroboration, his study guide prompts students to look for similarities and differences in the content of the documents. For example, he anticipates that students will notice discrepancies in the estimates of the number of casualties and that they will try to explain discrepancies by sourcing, especially noting when the texts were written in relation to the battle and on which side of the battle lines the authors stood. He has created partnerships so that students who may struggle with such a sophisticated analysis can lean on a stronger peer. During the partnership work he moves through the class, asking thought-provoking questions and complimenting students on their thoughtful analyses. As he passes Danielle and Andrea, Danielle expresses some frustration: "I don't know why we have to study the song. It doesn't tell us anything about the battle." Mr. Ramos acknowledges her frustration: "Does the fact that a best-selling song about the battle was written 150 years later tell us anything about it?" Danielle responds, "I guess that it means that this battle is really famous." Mr. Ramos agrees, "Yeah, I think that the Battle of New Orleans has become an important part of American pop culture. Is there anything else in the other documents that might support this idea?" Andrea makes a realization: "The textbook account does say that Andrew Jackson immediately became a national hero." Danielle adds, "And the painting with Andrew Jackson standing on top of the battle lines in the glowing sunshine holding a flag shows the same thing." Mr. Ramos offers praise and reminds them, "These are the kinds of ideas that you should record on your graphic organizer."

At the end of the class, Mr. Ramos calls for the class' attention and leads them in a discussion of the battle. Students enthusiastically share their version of the events, sometimes disagreeing with one another about specific details. Students debate the value of various texts. They are eager to share observations that they make about the sources and the content of the texts. They are curious about what others thought. The class members ask Mr. Ramos to tell them which document he thought was most reliable. When the bell rings to end class, the students are still debating as they leave the room. Mr. Ramos feels that students have a good understanding of the Battle of New Orleans and that they have practiced the important historical literacy strategies of sourcing and corroboration during the class.

HISTORY TEACHERS BUILDING HISTORICAL LITERACIES

There are tools of inquiry, habits of mind, strategies, and texts that are uniquely valued in history. The vignettes in this chapter illustrate four historical literacy strategies in detail: observation-making, inference-making, sourcing, and corroboration. It is unlikely that secondary students will receive instruction on how to use these strategies to negotiate or create historical texts outside of their history classrooms. Thus, it falls on the shoulders of history teachers to provide literacy instruction on the literacies that are vital in historical inquiry. However, the history teacher is not without resources in providing literacy instruction. School or district literacy specialists have expertise that a history teacher might lack. Through collaboration, the history teacher and content-area literacy specialist can develop lessons that support both content and literacy learning. But for this to happen, both the history teacher and the literacy specialist must share some common understandings.

First, the concept of text must be broadened to include all resources that are used to negotiate meaning within a content area. Historians use a wide variety of print and nonprint texts to construct understandings of the past. Many of the important texts in history, such as the artifacts in Vignette 1 and the painting in Vignette 2, fall outside of the traditional definition of text (i.e., words, sentences, paragraphs). These and other nonprint resources are important sources of historical meaning and are indispensable in the study of the past. Literacy specialists who fail to recognize valued nonprint resources as texts lose credibility in the eyes of history teachers. Moreover, there are several reasons why it makes sense to think of these resources as texts. Many of the same literacy strategies that are useful in working with traditional texts, such as inference-making, are equally useful in reading nontraditional texts. Similarly, many of the instructional strategies that are useful in teaching with traditional texts, such as explicit strategy instruction, are equally useful in helping students learn with nontraditional texts. By accepting a broadened notion of text, literacy specialists can collaborate with history teachers to help students learn to negotiate the various print and nonprint texts valued in history.

Second, history involves strategies, resources, and habits of mind that are unique. History teachers may be resistant to literacy specialists who enter their classrooms with a list of generic reading strategies that may not be useful in negotiating meaning with historically authentic texts. For example, instructing history teachers to teach before-, during-, and after-reading comprehension strategies when their students read a history textbook fails to address the historical literacy needs of secondary students. Instead, the literacy specialist might suggest that a history teacher supplement the textbook with multiple primary-source accounts and have students critique the textbook. Part of the role of literacy specialists should be to help history teachers to identify those literacies that are essential for negotiating historical texts and to develop a desire and the skills necessary to teach these strategies to students. Without the history teacher, the literacy specialist will struggle to identify authentic historical literacies engaged in by historians.

Third, without the literacy specialist, the history teacher might not recognize the value in teaching historical literacy strategies to students, nor will he know research-supported methods for teaching literacy strategies. Thus, without the support of a literacy specialist, a history teacher, whose focus is on teaching historical content rather than teaching historical literacies, might not take the time to teach strategies such as corroboration or sourcing. Collaboration between history teachers and literacy specialists can produce effective literacy and history instruction. For example, a history teacher might express to the literacy specialist a desire to teach students the strategies of observation-making and inference-making, skills that are recognized as important in the analysis of artifacts. The literacy specialist might suggest the teacher use explicit strategy instruction, an instructional method that the history teacher might not be familiar with. The history teacher and literacy specialist bring different, complementary areas of expertise that can merge to create powerful literacy lessons.

Fourth, and perhaps most important for history teachers to understand, they do not have to choose between teaching content or literacy. When the notion of text is broadened to include all of those resources that are useful in historical inquiry, and the notion of literacy similarly is broadened to include those skills needed to negotiate and create texts, literacy instruction becomes a natural part of history instruction. Teachers can spend time teaching the story of history as well as how it was written. And perhaps most important, history teachers are not expected to spend time teaching literacy strategies that are not relevant in historical inquiry.

CHAPTER SUMMARY

Historical literacy is the ability to negotiate and create interpretations and understandings of the past using documents and artifacts as evidence. History teachers are encouraged to build students' historical literacies by integrating literacy instruction into their teaching of the historical narrative. They are encouraged to introduce students to authentic historical texts. Through collaboration with literacy specialists, history teachers can build powerful literacy lessons that employ instructional methods such as explicit or implicit strategy instruction.

These lessons can help students use the sophisticated literacy processes necessary to work appropriately with the unique texts that are valued in historical inquiry.

REFERENCES

American Textbook Council. (1994–95). *History textbooks: A standard and guide.* New York: Author.

Britt, M. A., & Aglinskas, C. (2002). Improving students' ability to identify and use source information. *Cognition and Instruction, 20,* 485–522.

De La Paz, S. (2005). Effects of historical reasoning instruction and writing strategy mastery in culturally and academically diverse middle school classrooms. *Journal of Educational Psychology, 97,* 139–156.

Dole, J. A., Duffy, G. G., Roehler, L. R., & Pearson, P. D. (1991). Moving from the old to the new: Research on reading comprehension instruction. *Review of Educational Research, 61,* 239–264.

Driftwood, J. (1959). Battle of New Orleans [Recorded by Johnny Horton]. On *American originals* [CD]. New York: Columbia. (1989)

Ferretti, R. P., MacArthur, C. D., & Okolo, C. M. (2001). Teaching for historical understanding in inclusive classrooms. *Learning Disabilities Quarterly, 24,* 59–71.

Hall, G. S. (1883). Introduction. In G. S. Hall (Ed.), *Methods of teaching history* (pp. v–xiii). Boston: D.C. Heath.

Leu, D. J., Reinking, D., Carter, A., Castek, J., Coiro, J., Henry, L. A., Malloy, J., Robbins, K., Rogers, A., & Zawilinski, L. (2007, April). Defining online reading comprehension: Using think aloud verbal protocols to refine a preliminary model of Internet reading comprehension processes. Paper presented at the annual meeting of the American Educational Research Association, Chicago. Available at http://docs.google.com/View?docid=dcbjhrtq_10djqrhz

Nash, G. B., & Crabtree, C. (1996). *National standards for history.* Los Angeles: National Center for History in the Schools.

Nokes, J. D., Dole, J. A., & Hacker, D. J. (2007). Teaching high school students to use heuristics while reading historical texts. *Journal of Educational Psychology, 99,* 492–504.

Nokes, J. D., & Hansen, J. M. (2007, June). *Rethinking literacy in the social studies.* Paper presented at the Middle School Literacy Conference of the Center for the Improvement of Teacher Education and Schools at Brigham Young University, Lehi, UT.

Paxton, R. J. (1999). A deafening silence: History textbooks and the students who read them. *Review of Educational Research, 69,* 315–337.

Schug, M. C. (1982, November). Why kids don't like social studies. Paper presented at the annual meeting of the National Council for the Social Studies, Boston.

Stahl, S. A., Hynd, C. R., Britton, B. K., McNish, M. M., & Bosquet, D. (1996). What happens when students read multiple source documents in history? *Reading Research Quarterly, 31,* 430–456.

Stahl, S. A., & Shanahan, C. H. (2004). Learning to think like a historian: Disciplinary knowledge through critical analysis of multiple documents. In T. L. Jetton & J. A. Dole (Eds.), *Adolescent literacy research and practice* (pp. 94–115). New York: Guilford.

U.S. Department of Education. (2006). *2006 National Assessment of Educational Progress: History Assessment.* Institute of Educational Sciences, National Center for Educational Statistics. Retrieved March 12, 2010, from http://nces.ed.gov/nationsreportcard/main2006/2007474.asp#pdflist

Vacca, R. T. (2002). Making a difference in adolescents' school lives: Visible and invisible aspects of content area reading. In A. E. Farstrup & S. J. Samuels (Eds.), *What research has to say about reading instruction* (3rd ed., pp. 184–204). Newark, DE: International Reading Association.

VanSledright, B. (2002). *In search of America's past: Learning to read history in elementary school.* New York: Teachers College Press.

Wineburg, S. S. (1991). On the reading of historical texts: Notes on the breach between school and academy. *American Educational Research Journal, 28,* 495–519.

Wineburg, S. S. (1998). Reading Abraham Lincoln: An expert/expert study in the interpretation of historical texts. *Cognitive Science, 22,* 319–346.

Young, K. M., & Leinhardt, G. (1998). Writing from primary documents. *Written Communication, 15,* 25–68.

CHAPTER 5

(Re)Imagining Literacies for Music Classrooms

Paul Broomhead

As Ms. Henry plans music curricula for the coming school year, she meets with the school's literacy specialist, Ms. Po. Ms. Henry expects the usual pressure to add more book reading and emphasis on terminology to her music classes, but this year Ms. Po takes a different approach. She seems genuinely interested in music—particularly in how students get meaning through music. She focuses on two questions: In what forms does music content come to the students? and, How do students make meaning while interacting with these resources? Soon Ms. Henry perceives that Ms. Po honestly wants to understand and collaborate, and she finds herself enthusiastically explaining all of the ways people interact with music: they perform it, listen to it, contemplate it, and create it. Ms. Po returns to her initial question: "So, while students are interacting with music in each of these ways, with what exactly are they interacting?" Ms. Henry thinks hard. "Well, there are musical scores, musical instruments, conductors." "So, these are the sources of information for music students?" "Well, there are a lot more. There are musical performances, recordings, theory books, ensemble settings, and still more." Ms. Po gets excited. "Wow! I would love to learn more about all of these texts." At this point, Ms. Henry starts to see where this is going, "Texts?" "Yes, texts. The things you just mentioned are all things that your students negotiate and create in order to interact appropriately with music, right?" "Yes." "Then, those are your texts, and the ways students interact with them are your literacies." From this point on, both parties are hooked in the conversation—each of them engaged by insights drawn from the other's conceptions.

This chapter focuses on music literacy—what it is and why it is important. After defining music literacy, the chapter will present a teaching vignette based on Pygmy music and culture to demonstrate how music literacy instruction may be approached. Finally, this chapter will describe a successful literacy specialist/music teacher collaboration, including a discussion of how literacy specialists can help music teachers address literacy in music instruction.

DEFINING MUSIC LITERACY

Many people have written about music literacy, resulting in an array of definitions and instructional approaches. The most pervasive use of the term *music literacy* treats music notes and rhythms as components of a musical language to be decoded, and focuses primarily on the ability to read musical scores (Bartle, 2003; Collins, 1999; Gordon, 1993). From this perspective, accurate reading of scores—interpreting pitches and rhythms—appears to be a primary behavior of musically literate people. This type of literacy has enjoyed the attention of many within music education (Cassidy, 1993; Demorest, 1998; Elkoshi, 2004).

Some writers in music education use literacy-related terminology to talk about a more expansive view of music literacy—referring to musical interactions as music "discourse" (Barrett, 1997) and as "reading" and "writing" of musical "language" (Livermore, 1997). Music literacies in this conversation include capabilities beyond the realms of language (Levinson, 1990). Writings such as these that expand the definition of music literacy beyond the deciphering of music symbols are few, but are helpful in providing a context that is friendly toward the recasting of music education in terms of literacy, as this book invites.

Music literacy may be defined broadly as the ability to interact (perform, listen, contemplate, and create) appropriately with musical texts. Meaning-making comes through discipline-appropriate negotiation and creation of these texts. Music texts may include words but usually involve resources that are quite independent from written language. Consider the importance of a musician's ability to gain insight from a recording, respond to a conductor, participate appropriately with an ensemble, use space on a stage, and so on. Musical instruments, while used by experts primarily as tools to create texts, require such complex interactions with their players that even professionals must continue to carefully "read" them as they play.

Each of the four interactions referred to in this chapter are promoted by the National Standards for Arts Education. There are nine standards for music that encourage not only singing, playing, and reading music (*performing*), but also analyzing and evaluating music (*listening*), understanding music in relation to history, culture, and other disciplines (*contemplating*), and composing and improvising music (*creating*) (Music Educators National Conference, 1994). This chapter supports the notion that music literacy is important in all of the ways characterized by the national standards—performing, listening, contemplating, and creating—and that music literacy instruction should address all four.

A MUSIC LITERACY TEACHING APPROACH

The lens of literacy focuses our attention on a broad range of texts, resulting in two questions to guide our instruction. First, "What are the texts students need to negotiate and create in order to maximize meaning from the four interactions with music?" And second, "What do students need to know and be able to do in order to effectively negotiate or create a given text?" Music teachers and literacy specialists need to understand that since all interactions with music are interactions with a music text of some kind, the literacies associated with those texts define students' ability to make meaning through music. Addressing literacy, then, is not just an enhancement to music education—it is crucial to it.

The following vignette portrays instruction that might follow when Ms. Po has succeeded in helping Ms. Henry identify texts and literacies in all types of musical interactions (performing, listening, contemplating, and creating).

After consulting with Ms. Po, the school's literacy specialist, Ms. Henry considers how she can help her students become more able to negotiate and create texts while performing, listening to, contemplating, and creating music. Recently, Ms. Henry was impressed by a conference presentation where she learned about the music and culture of Central African Pygmies. She feels that the richness of this music and its contexts would hold opportunities for students to develop music literacies in all four types of interactions. She reflects on the aspects of Pygmy music and culture that were so meaningful to her: living circumstances, aspects of community leadership and interaction, role of music in Pygmy life, earthy vocal tone of the singers, layering of musical features, social balance that infuses the music, and so on. She begins identifying the texts that brought these aspects to light for her, and her own literacies that helped her make meaning of the texts. Excitedly, she checks in with Ms. Po again, who helps her identify even more texts, and then she plans her unit and calls it "Pygmy Perspectives."

A month later Ms. Henry's music room is brimming with a sea of sounds—excited talking, singing, percussive clatter, and other sound effects—coming from every direction in an incessant current of creative energy. There are several small groups of secondary general music students each anxiously planning its performance of an original musical composition created over the past few days. They have labored to incorporate aspects of Pygmy music and society, such as egalitarianism, flexibility, cooperation, and emotional freedom, into the process of creating the composition.

In one corner of the room, two students have split off from their group to practice vocal drum sounds, while the other four are standing in a close huddle and are adding a harmony part to the melody they wrote the day before. In another part of the room, the group is sitting in a tight circle—some clapping, some stomping and slapping their sternums, and others making vocal sound effects. Another group, in the farthest corner, is practicing with recorders, bongo drums, and a wood block.

Ms. Henry spots a group that is somewhat quieter than the others. She walks over and asks about their performance readiness. They have decided to use country western as their genre, with two guitars, a fiddle, two kazoos, and washboard percussion. The guitarists are not advanced enough to play anything but chords, and the group is worried about achieving "egalitarianism" in their performance (referring to the need for all participants to contribute equally). Ms. Henry asks, "What is required for the guitar part to feel equal to the others?" "Well, we're gonna have to have the attention on us for a little bit," says one of the guitar players. Ms. Henry responds, "Not necessarily. Think about this. It's true that you ought to have more than one thing you do because you have to achieve 'flexibility' too, but think about an ostinato. It is never the prominent part, but it's just as important as any soloing over it." Ms. Henry continues, "But I noticed in the folk ensemble video you were watching yesterday that the guitarists had more than one rhythm. They broke out for a few seconds here and there and did a more active rhythm. Let's see you try a couple of different rhythms. Now, you kazoos could take some rhythmic cues from the guitars and play off of them. Then we'd see some 'cooperation' too. You guys need to get practicing, though, because you have to be comfortable enough to really let loose tomorrow in order to achieve 'emotional freedom.'" Ms. Henry continues from group to group, looking for the aspects of the Mbuti Pygmy tribe in Central Africa that they've studied over the past several days. The performance is tomorrow!

The vignette provides demonstrative material for a discussion of each of the four types of musical interaction (performing, listening, contemplating, creating) and of how the two guiding questions presented earlier might be addressed: (1) What are the texts students need to negotiate and create in order to maximize meaning from interactions with music? and (2) What do students need to know and be able to do in order to effectively negotiate and create a given text? These two questions provide the format for the following descriptions of this process.

Performing

Texts where performance is one of the central interactions often include a musical instrument (including voice), a musical score, a conductor, or a performance setting such as a practice room, stage, or ensemble. Even one's mental and physical state can become a text to traverse before or during a performance.

Performing texts demand practice opportunities and instructor feedback. For example, a general music teacher may require students to gain a basic proficiency on a new instrument. After ascertaining what instrument students have access to and, perhaps, accumulating some instruments for the school, the teacher may assign students to do some research on the background of the assigned instrument and then, over the course of a semester, learn certain scales and a few simple songs from the folk literature or some other source that is appropriate for a particular instrument. The texts that need to be negotiated in order to maximize meaning during the performance interaction are the instruments themselves and any writings encountered during the research. The associated literacies include traditional word reading, but the primary literacies focus on the negotiation of a musical instrument and the creation of sounds that are appropriate for the context, including correct pitches and durations as designated in the musical score, correct intonation, appropriate tone quality, and so forth.

In the Pygmy Perspectives vignette, the performing-oriented objective was that students develop the ability to render an authentic performance of their Pygmy-inspired musical creations. The texts used were performances of others, the ensembles in which students were working, and any instruments used for the performance of their composition (including voice and other parts of the body). The literacies included the ability to (a) incorporate strategies and skills from authentic performances into a personal performance, (b) function within the social and musical dynamics of a small ensemble, and (c) operate a musical instrument with some facility.

In order to address performing literacies in the Pygmy Perspectives unit, Ms. Henry has students prepare their performances in small groups that constitute ensembles. She has students select an authentic genre within which to situate their performance. They study closely at least one performance within that genre. They must agree upon one or more specific performance-related strategies or skills to incorporate into their performance. (For example, they may identify a strumming technique, a formation, a style of leading the group, and so on.) The students spend time practicing performance strategies they've selected and developing the facility needed on the instruments to be used. The culminating activity is the students' performance of their group musical compositions in as authentic a manner as possible.

Listening

Texts where listening is one of the central interactions are mostly recorded and live musical performances of various kinds. Other texts may include listening maps and other listening guides, environments where performances occur, and various sounds one encounters in everyday life.

Here again, teachers provide frequent opportunities for musical interactions that give emphasis to listening and watching. For example, a choir teacher may regularly play vocal music from diverse musical cultures and have students describe the vocal tone. The texts are the recordings, and the negotiation of the texts includes opening the mind to unfamiliar music, identifying vocal timbres, and applying tone/timbre-related vocabulary to the various sounds.

The listening-oriented objective in the Pygmy Perspectives unit was that students develop the ability to hear and make sense of formal aspects and societal influences in Pygmy music. The listening texts used were sound recordings and live performances of peers at the end of the unit. Specific literacies included the ability to (a) recognize contrasting features in Pygmy music, (b) hear characteristics that correspond to societal characteristics, and (c) recognize influences of Pygmy music and culture in other types of music.

In order to address listening literacies, Ms. Henry plays a recording of one musical piece while she introduces students to the Pygmy culture through pictures. Then, after her discussion on societal characteristics (such as egalitarianism, cooperation, and flexibility), she plays musical excerpts that depict each of the characteristics in sound as she describes them to students. Later in the unit she has each small group watch and listen to a performance from its selected genre.

Contemplating

Texts where contemplation is one of the central interactions frequently involve traditional writings about music history, culture, music theory, and philosophy. Other traditional texts might be created through journaling or other reflective writings. Nontraditional texts include verbal presentations, demonstrations, musical scores, visual images, and performances.

Teachers concerned with contemplating music literacy will regularly provide opportunities to interact with these texts and give guidance and feedback. For example, a band teacher might focus students' attention on the form of a musical score being rehearsed and assign students to decide what impact it has on the large-scale dynamic shaping of the piece. The text is the musical score, and this instructional activity would nurture two associated literacies—the ability to identify formal structure in the piece and the ability to glean insights about musical shaping according to those structural features.

In the Pygmy Perspectives unit, the contemplation-oriented objective was that students develop an understanding of Pygmy culture through Pygmy music, and vice versa. The texts used were formal verbal and written descriptions of Pygmy society and recordings of Pygmy music. The literacies included the ability to (a) understand and appreciate societal characteristics by connecting verbal descriptions with visual images, (b) understand certain musical characteristics by connecting verbal descriptions with listening experiences, and (c) comprehend relationships between societal and musical characteristics.

In order to address contemplating literacies, Ms. Henry shows images of Pygmies while playing a recording of one musical piece, then turns the music down after a minute or two and gives a very brief introduction to Pygmy culture. She explains that these Pygmies live in Central Africa in the Ituri Forest, that they are referred to as Bambuti or Mbuti tribes, that they live in the forest for most of each year, and that they are very small, around 4 feet tall.

Ms. Henry then reads brief excerpts from a handout that she obtained at the conference where she discovered her interest in Pygmies. The handout describes characteristics of their society. For example:

> Specialization is likewise informal in the Pygmy community. All share the camp's main duty of hunting, particularly in the net-hunting groups. Beyond this, some may have recognized talents, such as storytelling, or singing, but these individuals do not occupy formal positions in the community, such as "storyteller," or "singer," nor are others discouraged from telling stories, or singing.

Afterwards, Ms. Henry reads additional excerpts from the handout describing how the same characteristics can be found in Pygmy music. After each of the excerpts she plays music that manifests in sound each of the aspects she is highlighting and has students describe what they hear in relation to these aspects. Finally, the class discusses examples in European musical tradition where the characteristics of Pygmy music are present. With guidance from Ms. Henry, students also note examples of music where these characteristics are noticeably absent.

At the end of the entire unit, Ms. Henry follows up all instructional activities by requiring a written group report of the experience. Students describe in detail how their group incorporated aspects of Pygmy music and society both into their music and into the process of creating and performing it. She ends the unit with a class discussion in which students identify the texts and literacies involved in the activity and discuss how those literacies might influence their ability to act appropriately in future musical interactions.

Creating

Texts encountered while interacting creatively with music involve both static and animated resources. Some common static texts encountered during creative activities include representations of the music notation system, instruments used for improvisation, and musical scores to which expressive deviations are added. Animated texts include ensembles, chord patterns, or any musical environments in which improvisation takes place.

Opportunities for students to act creatively abound in most musical settings. For example, an orchestra teacher may give students a packet with notation activities and provide regular instruction and practice on how to invent and transcribe diatonic melodies to paper, with the goal that students eventually will add their own simple "variation" to a "theme and variations" piece they are playing at a concert. The texts here are written instructions regarding notation, the verbal instruction of the teacher, and the theme and variations piece to which they are adding a variation. The associated literacies include basic notation skills and the ability to be melodically and rhythmically inventive.

The creating-oriented objective for students participating in the Pygmy Perspectives lessons was to develop the ability to create music informed by their understandings of Pygmy music and culture. The texts used were performances from various musical genres, music notation, and verbal expressions of creative ideas of others. The literacies included the ability to (a) reproduce aspects of compositions from various musical genres, (b) use notation to represent musical sounds, and (c) evaluate, respond to, and incorporate musical ideas of others.

In order to address creating literacies in the Pygmy Perspectives unit, Ms. Henry divides the class into small groups and assigns them to create a composition by completing the following steps and guidelines: First, students must, as groups, decide upon some authentic genre to provide a setting for their composition (vocal jazz, a cappella, drum circle, Mariachi band, country western ensemble, Pygmy tribe, etc.). Second, they must identify and listen to (or watch) a performance that is similar in character to the composition that they envision. Finally, they create a piece between 1 and 4 minutes long that incorporates insights from Pygmy culture and music. Notation is allowed but is not necessary.

The culminating activity is the students' rehearsal and performance of their group musical compositions in as authentic a manner as possible. Ms. Henry's influence is less overt during the creating activities than during the previous activities since her role has changed from presenting content to overseeing instructional activities that are, by design, primarily student-driven. However, although not specifically planned in advance, the feedback and guidance she provides during this activity is just as crucial as the overt instruction previously given.

THE LITERACY SPECIALIST/MUSIC TEACHER COLLABORATION

A healthy collaboration between a literacy specialist and a music teacher requires acknowledgment of each other's areas of expertise and a willingness to be taught. This applies equally to the literacy specialist and the music teacher. This section identifies roles for the literacy specialist and the music teacher by describing what each especially has to offer to the collaboration.

The Role of the Literacy Specialist

The literacy specialist's area of expertise is literacy, which ideally will include the broadened conceptions of text and literacy set forth in this book. His/her role, then, is to help music teachers understand this conceptual framework and to guide them as they apply these ideas to music instruction. Music teachers typically are not trained to view what they do as having to do with texts and literacies, and usually will need to rely on the informed literacy specialist to provide this perspective. In addition, music teachers will need feedback as they begin to identify texts and literacies and evaluate their instructional practices in light of the literacy framework.

In response to a given instructional challenge faced by a music teacher, the literacy specialist may see that a literacy-based principle might be helpful. For example, while planning instruction, a music teacher may become confused by the interwoven nature of the four musical interactions (performing, listening, contemplating, and creating). He/she understands that many, if not most, interactions with music actually incorporate all four types of interaction at the same time. Still, he/she recognizes a need to target certain interactions in instruction. An insight from the literacy literature may help to clarify this apparent complication in instructional planning. Kalantzis and Cope (2000) state:

These . . . ways of seeing meaning are never neatly linear. Often they happen simultaneously, or with one aspect in greater focus in the foreground but with the others still in the background. And the shift in focus can happen in all kinds of order, shifting focus frequently or slowly or irregularly from one aspect to another. (p. 242)

This statement referred to aspects of literacy instruction within the multiliteracy framework (New London Group, 2000), not to music. Nevertheless, this literacy-based insight is extremely useful in understanding the true nature of musical interactions. One interaction might be primarily performing, with listening as a major second feature, and contemplating and creating present but not prominent. Another interaction will involve primarily listening with a major component of contemplating, while performing and creating are minor components. This literacy insight improves teachers' ability to plan instruction by highlighting the interwoven nature of the four types of musical interaction, thus helping teachers more accurately identify which interactions are occurring in what balance. They then are better able to make purposeful decisions regarding the balance of texts and literacies they target in instruction.

In a second example, music teachers initially may experience difficulty differentiating between texts and tools for creating texts. The literacy specialist, who is there to clarify concepts and definitions, can help the music teachers with these types of distinctions by helping them focus on the purpose of the interaction with the object. A text is a resource whose primary function is to provide content. A tool is used to negotiate and create texts. For example, while a stereo requires some knowledge to operate, it is primarily a tool used to play a recording—the text. A single item may be mostly a text at one point and a mostly a tool at another. For example, while a musical instrument itself is primarily a tool for professional musicians as they create music, it is also one of the most important and primary texts for novice and intermediate music learners, for whom learning to negotiate the instrument is the primary goal and the actual music created is secondary.

In the literacy specialist/music teacher collaboration, the literacy specialist should approach the setting as a learner. He/she should ask questions, eager to learn what the music expert has to say about music literacy. Then, he/she should provide feedback using the principles of literacy discussed in this book—all the while being careful to acknowledge the content and instructional expertise of the music teacher.

The Role of the Music Teacher

Texts and literacies are identified when the music teacher, not the literacy specialist, decides what resources bring content to learners and what skills and understandings are needed to make sense of the text. This activity highlights the importance of music teachers planning literacy instruction in music as opposed to the literacy specialist.

The teaching examples presented here, including Pygmy Perspectives, can really be conceived and taught only by teachers who possess the literacies being addressed in instruction. This is because the music teacher, not the literacy specialist, is an experienced music performer, listener, contemplator, and creator of music texts. Were the Pygmy Perspectives unit taught by a literacy specialist, the entire unit would be devoid of specific guidance and useful feedback. Therefore, effective literacy instruction in music must be both conceived and carried out not only by literate educators, but by literate *music* educators. In order to nurture a successful collaboration, literacy specialists must honor the role of music teachers in identifying texts and literacies and designing instruction.

CHAPTER SUMMARY

The perspective and practices presented in this chapter represent a new way of envisioning what constitutes a music education. All music resources are seen as texts. All skills and understandings needed to negotiate and create these resources are seen as literacies. Literacy specialists can help music teachers in ways that enhance rather than interfere with authentic music instruction. In successful collaborations, literacy specialists and music teachers can explore together the guiding questions of music literacy instruction: What are the texts students need to negotiate and create in order to maximize meaning from performing, listening to, contemplating, and creating music? What do students need to know and be able to do in order to effectively negotiate or create a given text? This expansion in the conception of music literacy serves to inform and improve both the effectiveness and balance of music instruction.

REFERENCES

Barrett, M. S. (1997). Music literacy: I hear what you mean: Music literacy in the information technology age. In J. Livermore (Ed.), *More than words can say: A set of arts literacy papers* (pp. 40–52). Melbourne, Australia: University of Canberra.

Bartle, J. A. (2003). *Sound advice: Becoming a better children's choir conductor.* New York: Oxford University Press.

Cassidy, J. W. (1993). Effects of various sight-singing strategies on non-music majors' pitch accuracy. *Journal of Research in Music Education, 41*(4), 293–302.

Collins, D. L. (1999). *Teaching choral music.* Upper Saddle River, NJ: Prentice-Hall.

Demorest, S. M. (1998). Improving sight-singing performance in the choral ensemble: The effect of individual testing. *Journal of Research in Music Education, 46*(2), 182–192.

Elkoshi, R. (2004). Is music "colorful"? A study of the effects of age and musical literacy on children's notational color expressions. *International Journal of Education and the Arts, 5*(2), 1.

Gordon, E. (1993). *Learning sequences in music: Skill, content & patterns.* Chicago: GIA Publications.

Kalantzis, M., & Cope, B. (2000). A multiliteracies pedagogy: A pedagogical supplement. In B. Cope & M. Kalantzis (Eds.), *Multiliteracies: Literacy learning and the design of social futures* (pp. 239–248). New York: Routledge.

Levinson, J. (1990). Musical literacy. *Journal of Aesthetic Education, 24*(1), 17–30.

Livermore, J. (Ed.). (1997). Introduction. *More than words can say: A set of arts literacy papers* (pp. 5–11). Melbourne, Australia: University of Canberra.

Music Educators National Conference. (1994). *National standards for arts education.* Reston, VA: Author.

New London Group. (2000). A pedagogy of multiliteracies: Designing social futures. In B. Cope & M. Kalantzis (Eds.), *Multiliteracies: Literacy learning and the design of social futures* (pp. 9–37). New York: Routledge.

CHAPTER 6

(Re)Imagining Literacies
for Technology Classrooms

Steven L. Shumway
Geoffrey A. Wright

Within the technology education profession, the term *literacy* has several meanings. Because technology teachers are familiar with literacy across the curriculum initiatives, it is not surprising that they generally equate literacy to fluency in reading and writing printed texts. However, with the development of the Standards for Technological Literacy: Content for the Study of Technology (International Technology Education Association [ITEA], 2000), technology educators have focused their teaching efforts on helping students develop *technological literacy*, or the ability to use, manage, assess, and understand technology in a technological society.

Implicit within the concept of technological literacy are the broadened definitions of text and literacy introduced in Chapter 2. To be technologically literate, students must be able to negotiate and create content-specific texts in discipline-appropriate ways in order to engage in technology-related activities. Examples of these content-specific texts in technology education include sketches of design ideas, schematic diagrams, and orthographic drawings of a device. For each of these texts, there is a specific literacy that students need to be taught. Unfortunately, many technology teachers have a notion of content-area literacy that is limited to printed texts and thus are not explicitly aware of other texts central to technological literacy.

The purpose of this chapter is to demonstrate how broadened definitions of text and literacy apply in a technology education setting. Additionally, we provide literacy specialists with recommendations for helping technology teachers to recognize the texts their students must read and write, and to design literacy instruction that meets technology students' literacy needs.

TECHNOLOGICAL LITERACY

There is a growing importance of and dependence on technology in our society. Consequently, many individuals advocate the need for the general populace to understand and use technology in ways that are appropriate and beneficial. According to the National Research Council (2002), a technologically literate citizen should demonstrate certain characteristics related to knowledge of, ways of thinking and acting with, and capabilities associated with technology. A discussion of these concerns led to the development of the Standards for Technological Literacy (ITEA, 2000). These standards and their associated benchmarks were developed by groups such as the National Science Foundation, National Aeronautics and Space Administration, National Research Council, and National Academy of Engineering, in cooperation with the ITEA.

The Standards for Technological Literacy (STL) consist of 20 standards that for the purposes of this chapter can be grouped into three main categories: traditional core content, the design process, and societal impacts of technology. The first category focuses on what students should know and be able to do in relation to the traditional core content areas of manufacturing, construction, transportation, power and energy, medical, information and communication, and agricultural and bio-related technologies. Because many technology teachers have expertise in one or more of these areas, it is easy for them to develop units and lesson plans in these areas. Consequently, many of the activities found in current technology education classrooms are strongly focused on these traditional core content areas.

The second STL category outlines the design standards that describe the skills and understanding that a student should possess in order to engage in the engineering design process. This engineering design process is a set of procedures that engineers and technologists typically employ when designing technological systems or artifacts that solve a problem or meet some type of human need or want. While there are many variations of teaching the engineering design process in a technology education classroom, they typically involve students being able to perform the actions of identifying a problem, conducting research, generating ideas, identifying requirements, selecting a possible solution, and then building a model or prototype to test and evaluate the solution.

Many technology teachers struggle with exactly how to incorporate engineering design into their classrooms. Instead of teaching and engaging their students in the design process, many teachers simply provide students with a step-by-step script of how to complete a project from conception to completion. For these teachers, it is much easier to give the students plans for a project and then have them complete the project in a "lockstep" fashion, rather than to teach the students how to engage in engineering design.

The final STL category focuses on teaching about and helping students understand the impacts of technology on our society. These impacts include the implications of the appropriate and ethical use of technology processes and artifacts; the effects of technology on the environment; the social, economic, and political effects of technology on our society; the role of society in the development and use of technology; and the influence of technology throughout history (ITEA, 2000). This particular category of the technology standards is a weakness of many technology education curricula, as witnessed by the lack of lessons and activities that incorporate this content. For example, students in most technology education classrooms will learn how to build and program robots, but seldom is there a discussion of the history of robotics, the social impacts of robotics on the economy, or the cultural, ethical, and environmental impacts of robotics on society.

In order to fully teach and model technological literacy, technology teachers need to address all three categories of the technological literacy standards. To do this, we recommend that technology teachers continue to engage students in activities related to the traditional core content areas of manufacturing, communications, construction, and power and energy. However, instead of giving students specific project plans, teachers instead can provide students with opportunities to identify technological problems and then engage in the engineering design process to develop solutions to these problems. Furthermore, during each design cycle, teachers can encourage students to pause and consider the potential impacts of their design, as well as other technologies, on our society.

Providing opportunities for students to learn content in all three categories may, nevertheless, be insufficient if technology teachers do not also help students learn to read and write the texts that are essential for participation in the technology classroom. We provide the following vignette to illustrate how technology teachers might consider and address their students' literacy needs as they engage students in learning traditional core content, employing the design process, and considering societal impacts of technology.

Vignette: Mrs. Johnson, the technology and engineering teacher, is having a problem with her high school students arriving late to her advanced electronics class. Before coming to class, students often go to the vending machines. The time involved for them to make their purchases exceeds the allotted time between classes. The resulting tardiness of the students disrupts class and negatively influences the learning of the class. Mrs. Johnson recognizes that although this is a problem, it also presents a unique opportunity for her to help her students engage in and better understand the engineering design process, which is an important part of the technological literacy standards. She presents the situation to the class in order to identify the issues related to the problem and to brainstorm possible solutions. As a class, the teacher and students identify and list associated problems related to the vending machine dilemma on a whiteboard. The list ranges from students not eating nutritious breakfasts, to not enough time between classes, to an inadequate number of vending machines, which causes long lines.

As it is improbable that the school principal is going to allot more time between classes, or that the class will be able to change students' eating habits, the class settles on the problem of not enough vending machines. Students are then put into engineering groups where they brainstorm potential solutions to the identified problem. Following their collaborative brainstorming experience, the students are asked to present their solutions to the class while the teacher records their ideas on the whiteboard. Their solutions include the following:

- Eliminate vending machines altogether
- Purchase more vending machines
- Place vending machines in each classroom
- Provide alternative healthy snacks in the lunchroom

Mrs. Johnson then directs a class discussion in which the class is asked to choose a potential solution to the problem, with the additional requirement that the solution be related to course material and can be designed using classroom resources. In this case, the students select the solution of placing a vending machine in each classroom as a possible solution to the problem. The cost of a new machine is explored, but since cost is prohibitive, the decision is made to design and build a class vending machine using materials available in the technology and engineering lab. In order to be successful, students need to apply what they previously learned to new contexts as they progress through the engineering design process.

To start, Mrs. Johnson discusses with the class the engineering design process and introduces the decision matrix engineers often use as they engage in this process. The engineering design process involves students sketching their initial design ideas, conducting research to determine the electronic and mechanical systems needed to make a vending machine, and then designing, building, and evaluating their solutions to the problem. Mrs. Johnson reminds the students that when trying to determine which design idea to implement, engineers use a logical process to evaluate the strengths and weaknesses of each idea against predetermined criteria. Mrs. Johnson then has the students use the decision matrix (see Figure 6.1), which is a simplified version of what an engineer might use, to evaluate each of their design ideas. Students compare their ideas against a set of design criteria, assigning a "+" to ideas that match the criteria well, a "0" to those that are neutral, and a "−" to those that do not address the criteria. The idea with the highest score is the solution they will implement. This enables them to better choose an idea that can be successfully implemented.

As students progress in the design process, Mrs. Johnson leads the class in discussions of content-specific topics, such as digital electronics, the use of schematic diagrams to represent circuit configuration, microcontrollers, servomotors, basic mechanisms, the concept and use of patents, and the impacts of technology on society. In addition, Mrs. Johnson requires her students to peruse print materials on the Internet and in current electronics magazines

FIGURE 6.1. Decision Matrix

	Cost	Time	Practical	Materials	Total
Idea A	+	0	+	+	3
Idea B	+	0	−	+	1
Idea C	−	+	−	0	−1
Idea D	−	+	−	0	0

to see examples of how others use microcontrollers and servomotor applications. Mrs. Johnson plans lessons on the various topics and then teaches these lessons using multiple instructional methods and strategies (e.g., direct instruction, guided inquiry, cooperative learning, and just-in-time instruction).

After completing their preliminary research, students collaborate as small groups to develop their own designs, with the option of patenting unique design ideas. If groups want to use another group's patented design, bonus points are awarded to the group with the patent. As the students continue to refine their design ideas, Mrs. Johnson takes time to lead the class in discussions regarding the social, economic, and historical aspects of technology, including the importance of patents, and the positive or negative consequences of vending machines in schools. In addition, students conduct a survey of the school's student body to determine what types of items are to be placed in vending machines. An analysis is performed to determine costs and how profits will be used.

Students make a working prototype of their design and a portfolio consisting of various texts common in engineering design, such as sketches of their initial design ideas, a pictorial diagram of the final model, a schematic diagram outlining the function and flow of the vending machine, an operating instruction manual, a problem-solving log (e.g., a list of problems encountered as well as the solutions to the problems), a copy of the computer program used to run the vending machine, evidence of patents, and a list of resources used. Students then present their working design to nonengineering individuals (fellow students, their parents, and school administration) and resident experts (invited visiting engineers, manufacturers, and business owners).

THE USE OF TEXTS IN A
TECHNOLOGY AND ENGINEERING CLASSROOM

This vignette, based on an actual teaching experience, represents an ideal supported in the technology and engineering education profession in which students learn traditional core content, engage in the engineering design process, and consider the impacts of the technology they design. As students engaged in these three processes, they created and interacted with many types of text. Some of these important texts were traditional print materials. For example, students read teachers' notes, data manuals, and their textbooks in order to learn about stepper-motors, microcontrollers, the social impacts of technology, and other related engineering content. On the other hand, students also depended heavily on nontraditional texts as they sought to convey meaning and complete their designs. These nontraditional texts included schematic diagrams, component codes, sketches of design ideas, and drawings of the finished design.

The idea that these items should be considered as "texts" is supported by the notion of text being any object that is imbued with meaning and used to negotiate or convey meaning (Draper & Siebert, 2004). Schematic diagrams and component codes can be considered texts because they help convey to students not only what components are needed in the design, but also the method of connecting the components for the circuit to work properly. Technologists and engineers have long used sketches and drawings to convey the meaning of their ideas to others and show how the mechanical components of a device are interconnected.

In addition to the texts referenced in the vignette, there are many other texts that technology and engineering students often are expected to read, understand, and create. These include charts and figures (e.g., spreadsheets and blueprints); graphic organizers and descriptors (e.g., Venn diagrams, taxonomies, and concept maps); mnemonic devices (e.g., methods of reorganizing information to make it more useful); mimicry (e.g., the ability to recognize properties of familiar objects, or standards that need to be kept in place for function, tradition, and regulation reasons); mental representations (e.g., the ability to interpret other versions/variations of a product and then make one's own); iconic representations (e.g., students' ability to understand and interpret symbols that are used to improve readability and recognition); and error and code reading/interpretation (e.g., students' ability to interpret a text prompt placed on the screen by a computer program stating errors in the program, and then to fix the code).

For these texts to be useful to students as they learn traditional core content, engage in the design process, and explore the impacts of technology on society, the students must have a certain literacy level, understanding, or skill set. Acting appropriately with a text means that the students possess both a working knowledge of how the text is to be used, and content knowledge (Norris & Phillips, 2003). For example, the students must be taught that schematics and other symbols used in engineering and technology provide them with visual representations of information and thus allow them to decode the print texts that accompany the symbols. Students then must learn to decode the meaning of each of the schematic symbols and its associated component. Finally, they also should understand the purpose of each component in a circuit and how these components are interconnected to make a working circuit.

Our broadened definitions of text and literacy represent a break with traditional ways of thinking about literacy in the technology classroom. Historically, technology students were not considered to be engaged in literacy unless they were working with traditional print materials, such as taking notes in class, reading textbooks and content-related magazines (e.g., *Popular Mechanics, Elektor Magazine*), or using technical manuals. Although textbooks, technical manuals, and magazines can expose students to various content-related issues and help build some literacy skills, their use does not explicitly help students understand or become familiar with the many other texts and literacies important to and found in technology classrooms. Furthermore, without fluency with these other, nontraditional texts, students cannot engage in learning in any of the three areas recommended by the standards. If literacy educators and technology teachers do not adopt broader definitions of text and literacy and begin to support technology students in reading and writing *all* of the texts encountered in the technology classroom, they inevitably will fail in creating a technologically literate citizenry.

RECOMMENDATIONS FOR IMPROVED COLLABORATIONS

The technology education classroom is an excellent location for students to develop literacy skills with both traditional print texts and a variety of nontraditional texts. To fully realize this potential, the technology teacher and the literacy specialist must work together to combine their expertise in designing appropriate and effective literacy instruction. The following are recommendations for literacy specialists when working with technology teachers.

Motivating Traditional Print Literacy

Literacy specialists should recognize the unique opportunity that technology education curricula offers for students to develop reading and writing skills with traditional print texts by investigating topics that are interesting to them. Many times, students in a technology education classroom struggle with reading and writing traditional print texts. These students are often spatial learners who are gifted when it comes to psychomotor and manipulative skills, but lack interest in traditional reading and writing. The content and activities encompassed within technology education provide wonderful opportunities for otherwise disinterested students to not only develop the ability to become literate in the texts unique to engineering and technology, but also to find the motivation to develop their ability to read traditional print text.

For example, in the vignette, Mrs. Johnson has the students peruse the Internet and electronics magazines to find examples of how others are using microcontrollers to control electro-mechanical devices. In requiring the students to engage in this type of activity, Mrs. Johnson provides support for students' use of traditional print text by providing them with an authentic purpose for reading. Additionally, once students become familiar with the associated vocabulary, their ability to read print text materials increases; consequently, they are able to use the newly acquired text understanding while designing and building their projects. Magazines that describe how to create a home audio system, technical manuals that help students understand how to use a video camera, or books that describe how to fix a motorcycle are examples of traditional print materials that students in a technology class might be highly motivated to read. Note that these print materials need to be more than just an available resource in the classroom library. To be most effective, the use of these materials should be required as part of the design process in each project. The teacher can further increase students' success in reading these texts by modeling for the students how to use these materials as tools for learning content material, and for effectively engaging the engineering design process.

Although some students might still need help with remedial reading and writing even after the teacher sets a purpose and models good literacy practices, opportunities to develop these skills increase if the technology teacher and literacy specialist create a need-to-know situation where students are intrinsically interested in learning. In the vignette, these need-to-know situations present themselves as the students finish their prototype and begin programming the microcontrollers and troubleshooting the operation of the electronic devices. For example, getting the students to read the programming technical manual is difficult before they experience a problem. However, once problems are encountered, the students' need-to-know desire is amplified, and the teacher can facilitate learning by referring students to print and nonprint materials that will help them troubleshoot their design problems. Additionally, as the students in Mrs. Johnson's class develop their patents, they will need to write them correctly and in a technical format, with their writing clearly representing their idea in a professional and industry-accepted style. Mrs. Johnson, an English teacher, or even visiting engineers can provide guidance to the students as they learn to write these technical documents.

Identifying Discipline-Specific Texts

Literacy specialists need to help technology teachers identify the texts unique to the technology and engineering discipline. The technology teachers will have a general idea that there are texts unique to their discipline that are important for students to understand in order to develop technological literacy. However, having someone outside the discipline help identify the texts and validate that these texts are important for students to understand will be informative and welcome. This can help technology teachers move from a latent to an active understanding of the texts important in their discipline.

The literacy specialist should visit the technology classroom to become familiar with the content of the class so that he or she can sit down with the technology teacher and together identify texts that are unique to the particular technology. For example, if a technology teacher is teaching a drafting unit, content such as the types of lines (e.g., object, hidden, center, and dimension lines) or the types of drawings (e.g., orthographic, isometric, and exploded) needs to be identified as texts unique to drafting that students need help reading and creating. Literacy specialists will be better able to help technology teachers identify texts in their instruction if literacy specialists visit the technology classroom and see which texts students are expected to read and write.

Designing Instructional Strategies

Literacy specialists should work with technology teachers to design instructional strategies appropriate for teaching the students the literacies unique to technology and engineering. The literacy specialists should understand that technology teachers have expertise in teaching technological content to their students, and in reading and writing the texts of the discipline, but they may need assistance in developing instructional strategies that enable their students to develop literacy with these texts. Additionally, technology teachers will need to develop the ability to help their students understand that texts have affordances and limitations, and that the appropriate use of a text may be dependent on the audience and context in which it is used. For example, in the vignette, the students were required to present their working design and portfolio to resident experts and nonengineering individuals. Although the use of a schematic diagram would be the best way to describe to a resident expert what was happening within the vending machine, if students needed to convey information to someone who was not literate in schematic diagrams, it would be best to use a pictorial diagram of the circuit rather than a schematic. Rather than hoping students will intuit which text would be the most appropriate to use in a given situation, teachers should explicitly teach the concept of when and how to use various texts to convey the meaning of content.

In the vignette, the teacher employed a mixed-method approach involving various overt instructional techniques (e.g., direct instruction and inquiry-based instruction) to guide learning by helping students better understand and use the texts encountered in the content being taught. Table 6.1 outlines a few practical instructional techniques literacy specialists can recommend to technology teachers that can positively influence student understanding, interpretation, and use of texts.

Utilizing the "Hands-On" Nature of Technology Classes

Literacy specialists should recognize and appreciate the hands-on nature of technology classes and work with the technology teacher to utilize and strengthen this aspect of the content area. Traditionally, technology education has embraced an educational philosophy and pedagogy based on hands-on, real-life activities rich in situated practice. This tradition has been heavily influenced by the educational philosophies of John Dewey and other supporters of pragmatism who espoused an emphasis on hands-on, real-life curricular activities (Barlow, 1967). The purpose of these types of activities is to enable students to view the meaning of content critically in relation

Table 6.1. Instructional Techniques

Technique	Description	Benefit
"Just-in-time" instruction	The teacher scaffolds learning activities at the moment that students need new skills or knowledge so the students can accomplish increasingly complex and difficult tasks.	These activities can motivate students to learn because students often can see immediate applications for the ideas and skills they are learning.
Class discussions, critical dialogues, and creativity brainstorming sessions	Students meet, collaborate, and debate possible ideas, using various texts such as a decision matrix to refine ideas and solidify decisions.	Often, working as a group can help students better understand the texts encountered in the class.
Group presentations and/or performances	Students use texts such as sketches, drawings, and diagrams to present information to their peers.	Students can develop a better understanding of the affordances and limitations of these texts.
Interactive activities	The teacher uses board displays, computer-based projects (e.g., gaming, Internet research), and writing (e.g., adding to a class wiki or blog) to provide students additional opportunities to work with content-related texts in different mediums.	These activities can enable students to evaluate, assess, and clarify their understanding of texts.
Metacognition activities	The teacher has students "think out loud" (or silently), in groups or by themselves, to create a mental representation that helps them define the text.	These activities can help students to critically frame their learning and gain a better understanding of texts.

to context and thus diminish the inevitable question, "Why are we learning this?"

Within the vignette are examples of the type of hands-on learning many technology education students experience. For example, students were placed into engineering groups that allowed them to simulate what it was like to be involved in engineering design. The ideas of developing portfolios, conducting market analysis, and filing for patents were added to enhance the concept of situated practice; this was done by providing the students a hands-on experience of authentic and meaningful social practices (Gee, 2000).

A hands-on approach to technology instruction not only supports good content instruction in technology, but also can enhance content-area literacy instruction. As demonstrated in the vignette, it is because of the hands-on activities in the technology classroom that students are compelled to interact with a variety of texts in discipline-appropriate ways. Participation in hands-on activities can motivate teachers to help students develop facility with these texts and encourage students to work at becoming literate. Also, engagement in hands-on activities can ensure that students develop literacies that will be useful to them in technological situations outside of the classroom. If literacy instruction is not embedded in ongoing hands-on activities in the technology classroom, there is a chance that the instruction will result in students interacting with technological texts in artificial ways that are at odds with how these texts are read and written by practitioners in the field. By situating literacy instruction within ongoing hands-on activities, teachers can increase the likelihood that students will learn the actual literacies in the technological disciplines and not an artificial school literacy.

Aligning with the Standards

Literacy specialists should help promote instruction that is in harmony with the Standards for Technological Literacy (ITEA, 2000). It is important for literacy specialists to understand that although these standards have existed and have been accepted by technology teachers since 2000, many teachers struggle to appropriately implement them into their curriculum. It seems that many technology teachers have not understood how to blend their content instruction with all three categories of the technology literacy standards, and instead have persisted in teaching only the skills and processes from the traditional core content. One of the purposes of the vignette was to demonstrate a curricular unit that incorporated instruction based on each of the three categories of the STL. In the vignette, Mrs. Johnson took a traditional technology content area such as electronics, incorporated the engineering design standards, and then developed instruction that allowed the students to consider the societal impacts of technology.

One of the functions of a literacy specialist can be to work with the technology teacher to facilitate this type of instruction format. For example, as technology teachers share curricular ideas, the literacy specialist might ask questions such as, "How might design opportunities be incorporated into this lesson?" or "What is the historical significance of this particular technology?" The literacy specialist and technology teacher also can work together to find engineering design opportunities right in their own school. Problems such as congestion of traffic as students leave the school, slow-moving lines in the lunchroom, or improvement of school facilities for students with special needs are examples of authentic engineering design opportunities.

Finally, literacy specialists can promote students' understanding of the societal impacts of technology by helping technology teachers find recent journal articles to aid in class discussions on the impacts of various technologies. Articles on renewable energy resources, advancements in medical technology, transportation issues, construction projects, genetically engineered food products, and the latest in communication technology are examples of potential topics of discussion. In doing this, the literacy specialist can aid the technology teacher in ensuring that multiple categories of the standards are covered and thus can increase student opportunities to develop technological literacy.

CHAPTER SUMMARY

In this chapter, we discussed how the broadened definitions of text and literacy presented as a theme throughout this book apply in a technology education setting. Using a vignette, we provided examples of texts specific to technology education classrooms and discussed the importance of students being able to negotiate these texts to achieve technological literacy. Finally, we provided recommendations to literacy specialists for how they might work with technology education teachers to recognize the texts their students must read and write and to design instruction that meets their students' literacy needs.

The content and types of learning activities encompassed in a technology education classroom provide excellent and unique opportunities for students to develop literacy skills with both traditional print texts and a variety of nontraditional texts. To fully realize this potential, the technology teacher and the literacy specialist should understand that by combining their efforts and expertise, they will be able to design appropriate and effective literacy instruction. In doing so, they will provide students with a greater opportunity to achieve the goal of technological literacy and be better able to function in a technological society.

REFERENCES

Barlow, M. L. (1967). *History of industrial education in the United States.* Peoria, IL: Bennett.

Draper, R. J., & Siebert, D. (2004). Different goals, similar practices: Making sense of the mathematics and literacy instruction in a standards-based mathematics classroom. *American Educational Research Journal, 41*(4), 927–962.

Gee, J. P. (2000). New people in new worlds: Networks, the new capitalism and schools. In B. Cope & M. Kalantzis (Eds.), *Multiliteracies: Literacy learning and the design of social futures* (pp. 43–68). New York: Routledge.

International Technology Education Association. (2000). *Standards for technological literacy: Content for the study of technology.* Reston, VA: Author.

National Research Council. (2002). *Technically speaking: Why all Americans need to know more about technology* (G. Pearson & A. T. Young, Eds.). Washington, DC: National Academy Press.

Norris, S. P., & Phillips, L. M. (2003). How literacy in its fundamental sense is central to scientific literacy. *Science Education, 44*(8), 714–725.

CHAPTER 7

(Re)Imagining Literacies for Theatre Classrooms

Amy Petersen Jensen

Theatre educators rarely discuss literacy instruction as a formal component of their classrooms. While good theatre teachers are always working to help their students understand a variety of theatre texts, the term *literacy* is seldom used to describe the ways that students encounter the texts in their classrooms. Often theatre teachers mistakenly believe that literacy is best left to English educators, even though their training as theatre educators is innately infused with literacy education strategies and goals—namely, helping students access, analyze, contextualize, and create theatre texts.

This chapter will first, identify the learning goals that theatre teachers have for their classrooms; second, describe ways that literacy specialists can help teachers meet those goals through a literacy framework; third, present vignettes that demonstrate explicit literacy instruction; and finally, use examples from the vignettes to discuss ways that literacy specialists and theatre educators might work together to help students create meaning from the materials they encounter in a theatre classroom.

LEARNING GOALS FOR THEATRE EDUCATION CLASSROOMS

To engage effectively with theatre educators, literacy specialists should be aware of the goals, values, and propensities of theatre educators. The

National Standards for Theatre Education can help literacy specialists understand the learning goals for theatre classrooms. These standards direct theatre educators to help students view and create dramatic stories, or imagined worlds, about human beings. In a theatre classroom these stories about humanity are developed through visual, aural, and oral means. The writers of the national theatre standards also assert that to help students develop theatre literacies, teachers should encourage students "to see the created world of theatre through the eyes of the playwright, actor, designer, and director." They emphasize, "Through active creation of theatre, students learn to understand artistic choices and to critique dramatic works" (Consortium for National Arts Education, 1994, online).

Because theatre texts are both written and performed, theatre educators have at their disposal a wealth of interesting print and nonprint texts that they use to engage students in active instructional exercises. Because of these goals for the theatre classroom, theatre educators:

- Value experiential learning,
- Appreciate the difference between print and nonprint texts, and
- Place importance on the lens through which students read and create theatre texts.

Experiential Learning

Theatre educators often have an affinity for experiential learning. Theatre instruction in many ways is designed to reflect Dewey's (1934) conception of aesthetic representation. Teachers support processes where the creative use of materials and the imaginative development of possible solutions to problems allow for experience that affords both pleasure and learning. They agree with Dewey that the "expressive object" (i.e., the play script, the scenic design for a play, the performed play, and so on) is only a part of their instruction. They see the artistic processes, or development through experience, as "the most intimate and energetic means of aiding individuals" (p. 336). They believe that students in a theatre classroom acquire knowledge and skills by doing, practicing, or performing (Cook, 1917; Jackson, 2008; Lazarus, 2004). Because of this underlying philosophy, theatre teachers regularly focus on the experiential.

Difference Between Print and Nonprint Texts

Theatre teachers appreciate the need for fluency with printed texts, but they also recognize the need to engage with nonprint texts. Well before education theorists and traditional literacy researchers argued that content-area teachers should recognize the multimodalities of student learners (Cope & Kalantzis, 2000; Jensen, 2008; Kress, 2003), theatre teachers were providing students with opportunities to explore the combination of resources, processes, functions, and conditions necessary to engage in theatre (Boulton, 1999; O'Neill, 1995; Taylor, 2003). Their valuing of the written word stems from the acknowledgment that the written play text is the basis of drama. Students in secondary drama classrooms are required to read, write, and even generate play texts. The National Standards for Theatre Education promote reading and writing of traditional and nontraditional play texts. For example, Content Standard 1 focuses on script development and encourages "writing through improvising, writing, and refining scripts based on personal experience and heritage, imagination, literature, and history" (Consortium for National Arts Education, 1994, online).

Even so, a student's facility with theatre texts must go well beyond the printed page. Students in drama classrooms must have the ability to negotiate and create nonprint texts, including performed plays, sets, props, costumes, lights, sounds, bodies, movements, and the interactions among all of these possible performance texts. Participation in theatre's meaning-making processes is dependent on this ability. Moreover, practitioners, and therefore students, attempt to use the impressions they glean from reading scripts to re-envision the printed texts (mostly plays) performed on stage. For example, Content Standard 7 calls on teachers to provide classroom settings where students "analyze, critique and construct" meanings from a variety of theatre texts (Consortium for National Arts Education, 1994, online).

Lenses Through Which Students Interact with Text

Theatre educators ask their students to see their negotiating and creating of theatre texts through a variety of lenses or perspectives. Theatre practitioners engaging with a theatre text may examine it from the director's perspective, the designer's perspective, the performer's perspective, and so on. For example, a theatre practitioner who specializes in directing might look at a play script and read it with the intent of developing a dramatic concept for a staged version of the play. When reading the written play text he/she would determine the play's structure, organize the work into units of action, consider the demands of the characters, and envision the space in which character interactions might take place. In contrast, a designer would read the play and consider what the play script indicates about the time period, the setting (location, geography, space), and the physical requirements of the text. Like the director, he/she would consider the characters' interactions with one another and within the space, but would be thinking about them while imagining potential lines, colors, rhythms, and textures that could be employed in the creation of the wardrobe or the settings described in the play script.

Theatre performers obviously take on roles. Sometimes they portray a character in a staged play, and other times they perform roles in process-oriented dramas where a print text is seldom used (Neelands, 2000; Nicholson, 2005; Taylor, 2003). In both cases the live performance activities (sometimes viewed by audiences and other times not viewed at all) become texts to be read by students. The physical bodies of the performers are used with intent. Oral expressions convey performers' objectives. Participants engage in nonscripted, improvisatory activities with one another, manipulating and negotiating the architecture and topography of the space as well as the meaning-making implications of gesture, expressions of intellect, and repetition (Bogart & Landau, 2005). The body, then, acts as a nonprint text using its architecture, intellect, and expression to represent characters, stories, emotions, and other subjectivities that need to be read and understood by viewers or other participants.

MEETING THEATRE LEARNING GOALS THROUGH A LITERACY FRAMEWORK

When literacy specialists understand the learning goals of the theatre classroom described above, they are better prepared to work together with theatre teachers. This understanding will guide them as they work to improve literacy instruction in theatre classrooms and to develop a literacy framework that is designed specifically for the theatre classroom.

As the specialist and the educator think about ways that they can accomplish the task of infusing literacy instruction into theatre content, they may consider a variety of literacy strategies that could enhance authentic literacy instruction in the theatre classroom. For example, theatre teachers working with a literacy specialist might find Gee's (2001) notion of situated language a good fit because it values experiential inquiry. Gee argues that the "comprehension of written and verbal language is as much about experience with [various] worlds . . . as it is about words" (p. 720). For Gee, successful reading of any text requires more than an understanding of vocabulary or comprehension strategies.

Literature is also about understanding situated actions, social languages, and general modes of discourse associated with the text that one is reading. The learner, then, becomes aware of, and eventually a proficient participant in, new communities of interaction by "combining and coordinating words, deeds, thoughts, values, bodies, objects, tools, technologies, and other people (at appropriate times and places) so as to enact and recognize specific socially situated identities and activities" (Gee, 2001, p. 721).

By identifying theatre-specific texts (i.e., plays, bodies, set designs, costumes, etc.) and then determining the meaning-making processes associated with those texts in the way that Gee describes, literacy specialists and theatre educators can begin to explore ways that they can incorporate more opportunities for students to think like theatre practitioners. They also can provide classroom conditions that allow students to critically frame the theatre texts, or understand each text's social context or purpose. In addition, theatre teachers will be better prepared to assess and improve the methods that they are already using to aid theatre students as they access, analyze, contextualize, and create theatre texts in their classrooms.

The following vignettes explore two theatre classrooms that are infused with explicit literacy instruction. The first is a theatre classroom that embraces traditional theatre practices and the teaching of professional theatre roles. The second is a classroom that embraces applied theatre principles, which uses theatre techniques to teach or explore social issues that affect students. The type of literacy instruction employed in both settings is not literacy as it traditionally is perceived by literacy educators (reading and writing comprehension) but is instead focused on negotiating and creating a variety of theatre-specific texts.

Because theatre texts are both written and performed, the teachers support students in reading and creating both print and nonprint texts.

In each scenario I imagine a classroom where a literacy specialist has helped the theatre teacher to:

- *Provide access to a variety of theatre texts.* For the purposes of this chapter, the term *access* refers to students' opportunities to identify and use texts. The notion of access includes the development of necessary skills that students will need in order to approach those theatre texts. This could include, but is not limited to, exposure to formal and informal theatre texts, an introduction to theatre-specific vocabulary, or a scaffolding exercise that aids students in the reading of a given theatre text.
- *Engage students in authentic theatre analysis activities.* Conceptions of theatre analysis described here are intended to offer students genuine theatre experiences in which they closely examine various theatre texts and are introduced to the possible ways that they might understand the components of those texts.
- *Aid students as they contextualize theatre texts and activities.* In order for students to understand theatre texts, they must examine contexts in which the texts are created and presented, assess the value of those texts based on acquired knowledge, and reflect on the merits or qualities of those texts as conduits of meaning.
- *Present students with opportunities to create legitimate theatre texts.* Finally, students must participate in creation exercises in which they utilize a growing knowledge of theatre texts and their accompanying literacies to make theatre, bringing into existence their own artistic vision through experiential learning processes.

Vignette 1: The drama room at Sundance Junior High School is awash with movement and conversation. Beginning drama students are investigating Robert Frost's poem "Never Again Would the Bird's Song Be the Same" as a performance text. During the course of this unit of instruction Mrs. Graham has identified the poem as a theatre text and has asked her students to put on their "dramaturgy hats." For the purposes of her class she has defined a dramaturge as an investigator who helps a theatre director move performance texts from the written page to the performance stage by making inferences and observations about the written text. Mrs. Graham has explained earlier in the week that the role of the dramaturge is to investigate performance texts from a variety of angles. Sometimes dramaturges will approach the text from a literary perspective. Other times they will seek out historical information about the text and eventually they will think about how the information they have gleaned about the text from a variety of sources might aid in the development of a visual and aural picture necessary to stage the text.

The students are about midway through the unit and have already worked together to develop a concept map in which they organized and represented what they knew or understood about the world of the poem. In addition, they completed a formal analysis of the poem during which they asked questions about the author's perspective and the characters, themes, style, and mood of the poem. In a class earlier in the week the students completed historical research about the author and the poem itself. The students gathered this information through an inquiry-based web quest assignment in which they explored possible answers to questions that they had formulated in previous class periods. Based on this information, the whole class dialogued about potential visual and aural approaches to the text. Mrs. Graham noted the variety of choices that the students could make in the staging of the poem based on the varied and unique research gathered in the groups.

Today the students are building on the information they have gathered about the poem as they consider ways that they (as dramaturges) could help a director convey the visual and aural world of the poem to an audience. To do this they are employing basic visual and aural design vocabulary that Mrs. Graham has introduced them to, including line, shape, color, texture, rhythm, tone, pitch, and value. Several self-selected groups split off to work on topics of investigation that developed out of the discussion they had as a whole class.

The first group is creating a visual collage that represents the lines, colors, and textures present in the physical world of the poem. To construct the collage they are gathering and combining pictures from magazines, paint swatches, and fabrics, and even drawing colorful images and words that project their sense of the visceral space depicted in the poem.

Another group is building a soundscape, a combination of sounds that they formed to evoke an immersive aural environment for the poem. Students have brought sounds (both electronic and natural) that were recorded on a class member's iPod and currently are trying to create and record some of the guttural sounds that they imagined while reading the poem but could not find to record before class. As Mrs. Graham listens to the recording she reminds them that all the sounds they create should grow out of their understanding of the original text. She asks them to consider what aspects of the text drew them to the sounds they are creating.

The third group is developing a series of living pictures, or tableaux, that depict the interaction of characters with the physical space described in the poem. The development of the tableau series leads the students to new questions about characters from the poem and their relationships with one another and also the world in which the characters reside. Mrs. Graham reminds the students that the still images also provide new knowledge about the lines, shapes, and rhythmic interactions between characters and the space they inhabit. She asks students to think about how that might affect their explanation of those images to the other groups.

Mrs. Graham notes the progress of each group, offers suggestions, engages in conversation about the group work, and eventually brings the class back together to share the visual and aural materials that they have developed. Once they have shared their material with the other groups, the students and Mrs. Graham determine which of the collected resources will best help them to stage the poem for a future class.

Vignette 2: In an advanced drama class at East Shore High School, Ms. Ashworth is teaching a unit of instruction in which her students explore the power of the body in conveying stories, messages, or social ideas. During this class period she is guiding the students through a series of image creation exercises that allow each of them to investigate ways that they can use their bodies to convey these ideas. Today they are focusing on how they might physically express types of oppression that they have experienced personally.

To accomplish this task she has introduced them to the concept of image theatre, a series of physical exercises designed to help them consider messages present in society, culture, and themselves. She explains that in these exercises they will use their own and others' bodies as clay, and that together they will "sculpt" statues or still images that represent their experiences, feelings, and ideas. She begins by asking the students to find a space in the room where they can work. She asks everyone to create a static pose that signifies a moment when they were oppressed or dominated by someone or something. She then invites them to mold or sculpt their own bodies into a pose or image that represents that situation, emotion, or idea. Ms. Ashworth encourages the participants to create these initial images without thinking deeply about them. She explains that image theatre relies first on the body and that by using their bodies to represent emotions, they might be able to more fully express the extent of their experience than if they had been asked to represent the same experience through spoken or written language.

Once the images have been created, she asks the students to examine their classmates' images. She points out that image theatre can be an investigation of potential truths through community discussion about the images. She gives students time to view several of their peers' images and then to verbally reflect on the possible meanings of each image.

Once this has been accomplished, she asks the students to form smaller groups in order to dialogue about one of the original images produced by a member of the group. She tells the students that an integral component of this part of the exercise is to consider ways that the image might be more fully understood by the larger community. She reminds them that like the creation of the original image, this dialogue also is primarily about exploring how the physical body portrays the experience. She encourages the group to use their own bodies to resculpt the original image and to portray their opinions on the issue of this particular oppression. Ms. Ashworth has students repeat this part of the process until students come to an agreement about how to best represent the emotional content of the original image.

The students, who previously have studied Augusto Boal's (1995) philosophy of theatre for personal and social empowerment when they read portions of his book *Theatre of the Oppressed*, are particularly engaged when Ms. Ashworth suggests that at this point they should work as a group to create a counterimage to the first one, or an "ideal image." This ideal image is formed when participants enact a second image where the oppression is overthrown. She instructs them that to accomplish this they also must create a transition action that projects an evolution from the reality presented in the first image to the intended or hoped-for change represented in the final or ideal image. When students ask why the transition between the real image and the ideal or counterimage is important, she explains that her intent is to encourage them to consider the many possible ways that they might overthrow the original oppression in reality.

She suggests that in this part of the exercise they can make the original image dynamic, or alter it to express different facets of the original oppression. She provides them with several ways to accomplish this.

- First: The students might incorporate a rhythmic movement that seems to be contained within the image. The rhythmic movement should come from the original static pose and give it life. This movement could inform the viewers even more about the theme of oppression, or provide the class with more information about the oppression and its counter or ideal image.
- Second: The groups could alter their images slightly so that each participant interrelates with the other people on the stage. Their poses could relate to one another in a way that creates a single perspective that encompasses all views and leads to images of the oppression overcome.
- Third: The members of the group might introduce a spoken phrase that compliments the performer making the movement and leads to the presentation of the ideal image.

The students discuss possible transition actions and counterimages, and determine the best way to physically perform a change from the original structure of oppression to the ideal image—one that reflects freedom from the oppression. Once they have decided on a course of action, they stage their images for the other class members.

CREATING MEANING IN THE THEATRE CLASSROOM

In the vignettes, we imagine two classrooms where theatre teachers have improved their content teaching by infusing it with literacy instruction. With help from a literacy specialist both Mrs. Graham and Ms. Ashworth explicitly teach their students to negotiate and create theatre texts.

Working with a literacy specialist, these teachers have consciously attended to the literacies of theatre-specific texts and genres. The following paragraphs examine aspects of both classrooms where literacy instruction occurred because of conversations between the content-area teacher and the literacy specialist. Each discussion models ways that literacy specialists and theatre educators might work together to establish curriculum goals that infuse literacy instruction into the meaning-making processes already present in these classrooms, helping students access, analyze, contextualize, and create theatre texts.

Helping Students Access Theatre Texts

Attending to literacy instruction in the theatre classroom helps educators focus on the variety of texts they might assist students in accessing. A literacy specialist might help theatre educators understand that a key question to ask when preparing to use literacy strategies in a theatre classroom is, "What are the theatre texts that students will encounter in this lesson?" By identifying the materials that will be explored as text, regardless of their status as print or nonprint resources, the literacy specialist helps the teacher provide a literacy focus for the classroom instruction that meets theatre content goals. With that focus in mind, the theatre educator can determine what the students have to understand to successfully negotiate or create the text at hand.

Both of the vignettes above have texts that are used in instruction. In the first vignette Mrs. Graham and her students engage with a print text, the written poem. In the second experience Ms. Ashworth and her students explore the body as a text. This, of course, is a nonprint text. In both cases identifying the poem or the body as text gives weight to the exploration of those texts for both the students and the teacher.

Theatre educators also can help literacy specialists by introducing them to theatre-specific codes for accessing texts in their subject matter. For example, when accessing a text in theatre settings, individuals often assume a role that determines their purpose for engaging with the text. Both Mrs. Graham and Ms. Ashworth help the students to access the texts they are investigating by providing the students with a particular theatre lens through which they can view and respond to the texts. Mrs. Graham asks her students to see the poem through the lens of the dramaturge. When doing this she explains the dramaturge's artistic role and the specific vocabulary associated with that role to aid them in their analysis of the text. In addition, she guides the students in a more focused exploration of the text when she explains the responsibilities of this role (making observations and inferences about the text in order to help the director stage the production).

Ms. Ashworth also asks her students to assume a creative posture through which they work to understand the text. She asks them to take on the role of performer/sculptor. She explains that in this role they will use their own and others' bodies to "sculpt" still images that represent their experiences, feelings, and ideas. It is through this theatre-specific lens that students can begin to view, interpret, and create the stories they encounter in the images presented.

Analyzing Theatre Texts with Young People

Literacy specialists and theatre educators can pool their resources to think about strategies for analysis that might best work in the theatre classroom. A literacy specialist can easily step in to offer traditional literacy methods, such as setting a purpose for reading, that would enhance instruction and further the students' investigation of a text. The more difficult task for the literacy specialist is to help improve students' theatre-specific literacies. As they work together, the question that the literacy specialist and the theatre teacher should ask each other is, "What do the students need to know in order to effectively negotiate the theatre text that they are studying?"

Mrs. Graham's lesson provides us with an example of this type of instruction. She has determined that her students will better understand the performed text if she scaffolds the meaning-making processes by first introducing print literacy strategies, borrowed from the literacy specialist, for engaging with the text. She then builds on the students' knowledge gleaned through participation in the traditional literacy strategies, using theatre-specific literacies that focus on embodiment, or the ability to imagine and create sounds, images, and characterizations based on the observations and inferences they have developed during the early stages of the unit. As she engages them in a performative analysis of the text, she also guides them in a theatre-specific analysis by asking them to determine how they can justify their artistic explorations through the original text.

Contextualizing Text in the Theatre Classroom

In discussions about theatre literacy, the theatre educator will have a stronger grasp of the fundamentals of contextualization in theatre practice than the literacy specialist will. The specialist should acknowledge this. Alternatively, the literacy specialist can act as a coach, helping the theatre educator to better see ways that his/her students can effectively contextualize the texts they are presented. Guiding questions for strategizing together about contextualization might include, "How can I help my students examine contexts in which theatre texts are created and presented?" and "What reflective strategies have I incorporated into this unit or lesson that aid students as they assess the context and value of those texts based on what they know?"

Vignette 2 provides us with an example of how examination and reflection strategies can appropriately engage students in an impactful discourse about the text they are exploring. In this vignette the text the students are exploring is the human body—their own performing bodies. Ms. Ashworth prepared the students to explore and contextualize their bodies by introducing the students to tools that promoted both engagement and evaluation. Specifically, she provided students with an academic context for their exploration of the body.

Prior to engaging her students in the image exercises, Ms. Ashworth introduced them to the theoretical writings of Augusto Boal, the theatre educator who authored the exercises. She also placed his work in a particular context by introducing students to the concept of critical theatre pedagogy (Boal, 1995; Freire, 1970), an approach to learning that asks participants to challenge dominant beliefs. Ms. Ashworth familiarized the students with Boal's notion that theatre tools can help individuals to deal critically with reality, and that their role as performers in this exercise would be to discover how to participate in the transformation of the various oppressions present in their unique worlds. Notably, she emphasized the importance of creating a safe space where people could feel comfortable performing and responding to the performance. This information provided an objective through which the students could explore their own image work.

Also, Ms. Ashworth implicitly established a pattern of action, evaluation, and reflection in the image work that supported the students' ability to assess and think about the creative activity. Students engaged with the text initially through a theoretical discourse (critical pedagogy). They then engaged with the images created by themselves and their peers. Ms. Ashworth directed them to expand on the image or show a variation on the image without using damaging critiques. Finally, after the exploration and discussion, they reinvented the original image to include several possible solutions to the oppression evidenced in the original image.

Creating Texts in the Theatre Classroom

Creation experiences occur frequently in the drama classroom. The literacy specialist can help the theatre educator to see how these experiences can help students practice their knowledge of theatre texts. The literacy specialist also can point out that creation experiences should be shaped by the literacy and learning strategies described above that aid students in becoming theatre artists. Questions and strategies that the literacy specialist and theatre educator have developed together in preparation for accessing, analyzing, and contextualizing texts also can ground the creative exercises. In addition to the questions developed through activities, the literacy specialist and theatre educator might interrogate the theatre lesson plans with questions specifically focused on the texts and literacies associated with creative products and processes by asking, "How do I encourage students to create theatre texts based on their prior knowledge of other theatre texts?" and "How might the creation processes my students experience in this lesson be enhanced by reflection about both theatre processes and the products that may be created through those processes?"

These creative products and processes are the culminating objectives of both literacy acquisition and great theatre instruction. They are achieved when access to a theatre-specific text is given through a process of text identification. This process of text identification can be enhanced by the value that theatre educators regularly place on experiential learning. Similarly, theatre educators' recognition and appreciation of print and nonprint texts lead to meaningful analysis of those texts; and the natural importance they give to viewing texts through a variety of lenses (or from varying perspectives or roles) leads to in-depth contextualization. In addition, the creation of texts provides opportunities for students to attend to the concerns of their audience and therefore to see the creative process as a dialogue between the creator and the intended audience. The creation of new theatre texts then becomes the climatic demonstration of both theatre literacy acquisition and theatre practice, which evidences a mastery of theatre texts and theatre content.

CHAPTER SUMMARY

This chapter outlines the need for explicit attention to texts and literacies present in theatre classrooms. Helping students to construct meaning with theatre texts is essential for good instruction. Theatre educators must help their students negotiate and create the texts they are using, if students are to fully learn the content or participate in authentic theatre activities. Literacy specialists can aid the theatre educator in these pursuits.

In addition, the chapter delineates the ways that literacy specialists and theatre educators can work together to infuse theatre classrooms with authentic theatre literacy instruction. To accomplish this, the literacy specialist must realize the unique concerns of the theatre classroom and encourage the theatre educator to develop lesson plans and implement instructional strategies that will better reveal the many print and nonprint texts within the content area. The literacy specialist and the theatre educator also must work together to discover the theatre literacy strategies that best help students access, analyze, contextualize, and create theatre texts. If this happens, the collaborative effort can have a significant impact on the theatre classroom and on the lives of the adolescents who study theatre.

REFERENCES

Boal, A. (1995). *Theatre of the oppressed.* New York: Theatre Communications Group.

Bogart, A., & Landau, T. (2005). *The viewpoints book.* New York: Theatre Communications Group.

Boulton, G. (1999). *Acting in classroom drama.* Portsmouth, NH: Heinemann.

Consortium for National Arts Education. (1994). *National standards for arts education: Theatre standards.* Retrieved from Kennedy Center for the Arts, Arts Edge, at http://artsedge.kennedy-center.org/teach/standards.cfm

Cook, C. (1917). *The play way.* Portsmouth, NH: Heinemann.

Cope, B., & Kalantzis, M. (Eds.). (2000). *Multiliteracies: Literacy learning and the design of social futures.* New York: Routledge.

Dewey, J. (1934). *Art as experience.* New York: Shocken Books.

Freire, P. (1970). *Pedagogy of the oppressed.* New York: Herder & Herder.

Gee, J. P. (2001). Reading as situated language: A sociocognitive perspective. *Journal of Adolescent and Adult Literacy, 44*(8), 714–725.

Jackson, T. (2008). *Theatre education and the making of meanings: Art or instrument*. Manchester, UK: Manchester University Press.

Jensen, A. P. (2008). Multimodal literacy and theatre education. *Arts Education Policy Review, 109*(5), 19–28.

Kress, G. (2003). *Literacy in the new media age*. London: Routledge.

Lazarus, J. (2004). *Signs of change: New directions in secondary theatre*. Portsmouth, NH: Heinemann.

Neelands, J. (2000). *Structuring drama work* (2nd ed.). London: Cambridge University Press.

Nicholson, H. (2005). *Applied theatre: Drama and performance practices*. London: Palgrave Macmillan.

O'Neill, C. (1995). *Drama worlds: A framework for process drama*. Portsmouth, NH: Heinemann.

Taylor, P. (2003). *Applied theatre: Creating transformative encounters in the community*. Portsmouth, NH: Heinemann.

CHAPTER 8

(Re)Imagining Literacies for English Language Arts Classrooms

Sirpa Grierson

Jeffery D. Nokes

Chris Crowe, an author and former high school teacher whose novel, *Mississippi Trial, 1955* (2003), is featured in this chapter, writes:

> In English language arts classrooms, my novel—and, for that, any novel—is merely a vehicle for engaging students in a rich variety of language arts experiences: discussing history and humanity, improving reading skills, increasing vocabulary, practicing critical thinking, improving writing, and many of the other sorts of activities that take place in an effective English class. (Grierson, Thursby, Dean, & Crowe, 2007, p. 80)

Why include a chapter in this book on how literacy specialists can better work with English language arts (ELA) teachers? Shouldn't every English teacher, like Crowe, be concerned with improving his/her students' literacies? Yes. But, due to a lack of consensus as to what constitutes English as a discipline, the English language arts standards (National Council of Teachers of English/International Reading Association [NCTE/IRA], 1998) are interpreted in multiple ways (Peters & Wixson, 2003). It is our contention in this chapter that current ELA instruction often falls short of the literacy instruction described by Crowe, endorsed by ELA standards documents, and promoted throughout this book. This instruction is possible, however, through collaboration between literacy specialists and ELA teachers. Consequently, we suggest in this chapter that literacy specialists must not assume that all ELA teachers have a strong background in or inclination toward literacy instruction. Instead, literacy specialists must include ELA teachers in their schoolwide efforts to provide rich literacy experiences for all students.

Our discussion opens with a description of the way things are, looking at three current models of ELA instruction. It continues with a vision of the way things might be if ELA teachers included a wide variety of language-based texts and language-based literacies in their language arts classrooms. This second part of the chapter highlights the ELA standards produced by the NCTE/IRA (1998), followed by an example of our (re)imagined ELA classroom described in a vignette. The chapter concludes with a description of how literacy instruction in an ELA classroom can be improved by teachers' adoption of the broad notion of texts and literacies advocated in this book and through collaboration between literacy specialists and ELA teachers.

THREE MODELS OF
ENGLISH LANGUAGE ARTS INSTRUCTION

Instruction in ELA classrooms typically follows one of three models: (1) a mastery model, (2) a cultural heritage model, or (3) a process model (Peters & Wixson, 2003). The controversy over these models has divided ELA instruction into competing orientations. Peters and Wixson ask the rhetorical question, "Which of these models will win the battle for the soul of the language arts classroom?" (p. 574). A brief description and review of each of these three models will show the advantages and disadvantages of each and why we believe their strengths should be combined under the ELA umbrella.

The Mastery Model

The mastery model of English instruction focuses on students' development of a collection of literacy skills. The reading process, defined narrowly, is broken down into a series of desired behaviors, such as identifying the verb in a sentence or finding the main idea of a paragraph. Lessons are designed to help students master each of these behaviors in a carefully controlled sequence. As mastery model classrooms often rely on packaged programs, teachers make few choices about the texts used or the lessons taught. The focus of mastery instruction is not literature, content, or processes involved in literacy; instead, the focus is on the mastery of a discrete collection of skills that are viewed as essential in traditional reading comprehension. There is no question that proficient readers need certain reading skills. Teachers who follow this model are committed to building those skills in their students.

However, we have several concerns with the mastery model of English instruction. Its values stand in stark contrast to ELA standards and the definition of literacy promoted in this book. The mastery model, according to Peters and Wixson, "does not have a K–12 scope and sequence [nor] is it connected to other ELA processes—writing, listening, speaking, and viewing" (2003, p. 574) and consequently lacks the real-world application required by the ELA standards. Instead of an expanded notion of literacy, which includes the ability to negotiate and create meaning with a broad variety of texts, the mastery model focuses solely on traditional print literacies. Additionally, the skills typically taught in mastery-focused classrooms exclude many literacies that are most basic in our efforts to help students have rich experiences with texts, such as those described by Crowe at the outset of this chapter. Skills associated with mastery teaching are decontextualized, that is, unconnected to real literature, rather than used in authentic situations. Many literacy advocates have been critical of this model. Yet the mastery model, made popular by behaviorist theories in the 1970s, is experiencing a surprising resurgence as schools and districts look for "teacher-proof" ways to improve students' test scores. As mentioned earlier, the mastery model does not provide guidance on the selection of texts, which is the primary focus of the cultural heritage model.

The Cultural Heritage Model

The cultural heritage model of English instruction promotes the study of the traditionally accepted literary canon. Literary works are selected based on their inclusion of the values, ideas, and histories that are part of the larger culture. Teachers have good reason to want to introduce students to the classics. They want their students to appreciate the universal themes and the beautiful language found in these works. They also want their students to recognize and understand the numerous allusions to the classics that are part of the culture of the educated. Thus, advocates of the cultural heritage model believe that to be truly educated a person must become familiar with "the" literary works that form the foundation of our culture. Some advocates of this model have produced lists that include all of the cultural elements that they believe students should know (e.g., Hirsch, 1987). In recent years, in an effort to make the canon more multicultural, it has expanded to include texts from multiple perspectives. However, in many class-rooms teachers build their curriculum around the same classics that they studied when they were in high school.

We have two criticisms of this model of English instruction. First, such a limited conception of text eliminates many of the texts that have become a basic part of adolescents' and adults' literate lives, includ-ing adolescent literature, and ignores what we believe are the essen-tial texts and literacies of the 21st century. Our second criticism of this model of English instruction is stronger than the first. In many cultural heritage classrooms, the expectation that basic literacy skills, and spe-cifically reading, will be taught as part of the curriculum is not pres-ent. Especially in high school, the focus is on literature and not basic literacy. Some may have the attitude that students will develop literacy skills naturally as they interact with classic texts. Ironically, the atti-tude of other cultural heritage teachers mirrors the attitude of many content-area teachers: Others are responsible for literacy instruction. Building students' literacy may be a by-product of their regular use of texts, but it is not an explicit objective of their instruction. In extreme cases, teachers in cultural heritage classrooms may become frustrated by students' limited literacies that result in their inability to access the canon. Unfortunately, some teachers' solution may be to transfer stu-dents to remedial courses rather than working to build their literacies, as such basic literacy instruction would distract from the study of the canon. The lack of literacy instruction in the cultural heritage model contrasts with instruction in process model classrooms.

The Process Model

The process model, so-called because of the desire to actively engage students in the reading and writing process, allows for a broader notion of literacies and texts. Unlike the mastery model, which is intended to produce automatic skills through repetitive drills, this model focuses on the development of strategic readers and writers, students who will-fully employ heuristics to aid comprehension and to facilitate compo-sition. Process model teachers recognize the need to provide regular overt literacy instruction that helps students become strategic in their reading. Additionally, process model teachers recognize the role of the students' experience in the construction of meaning with texts and they foster and value individual students' unique responses to text. They acknowledge that literacy is much more than discrete skills associated with reading. Instead, it includes the students' affective, cognitive, and social engagement with language in its various written and oral forms. The process model suggests that instruction be more practical in its con-cerns with literacy and its real-world applications, and it incorporates many of the current ELA standards (NCTE/IRA, 1998).

Unlike the cultural heritage model, the process model advocates that teachers select texts of various genres based on their relevance to students' lives. While the model itself provides little guidance about the texts students should study, we contend that this flexibility can en-large the curriculum. Sensitive teachers can select texts based on their students' cultures, interests, literacy needs, and worlds. Those texts may come from the canon, like *To Kill a Mockingbird* (Lee, 1960/2002), from current adolescent literature, like *Mississippi Trial, 1955* (Crowe, 2003), or from nontraditional texts, like the Library of Congress' Internet resources on the Civil Rights Movement (Campbell, Eichacker, Tousignant, Ricci, Woodward, Levine, & Hamilton, 2003).

We contend that these three models, the mastery model, the cul-tural heritage model, and the process model, should be integrated to create effective ELA classrooms. A literacy specialist who is aware of the models of belief and practice, as well as knowledgeable in the ELA standards, has a far better chance of being an agent of change in an English classroom. Under the umbrella of ELA standards, literacy specialists can draw from all three models to help teachers empower students with lifelong literacy skills.

THE ENGLISH LANGUAGE ARTS STANDARDS

In the secondary school, the term *English language arts*, first coined by Bostwick in 1935, refers to a student-centered, inquiry-based approach to literacy acquisition. In an effort to merge the theory and practice of literacy, national English standards have attempted to combine the three models under one umbrella—ELA. In fact, this merger leans curriculum toward the process model, which is, according to Peters and Wixson, more "ideologically mainstream" (2003, p. 574) and, we believe, best expresses the ELA standards and the process of becoming literate. It is both inclusive of the literacy needs of all adolescents and can be applied to literacy learning in all secondary grades.

The standards document recommends broadening the range of language-based texts used in ELA classrooms without entirely abandoning the traditional canon. Teachers are encouraged to use print and nonprint texts from many periods and many genres that build students' understanding "of themselves, and of the cultures of the United States and the world." Teachers are encouraged to include spoken, written, and visual texts, including artifacts. Further, the standards discuss literacies that students should build in their ELA classrooms. Teachers are encouraged to teach students to gather, evaluate, and synthesize data. Students should be able to consider their context and audience and adjust their spoken, written, and visual language according to their purposes. The standards encourage teachers to include vocabulary training and instruction that help students "apply a wide range of strategies to comprehend, interpret, evaluate, and appreciate texts" (IRA/NCTE, 1996, p. 25). According to the standards, literacies include the ability to draw upon prior experience, to generate ideas and questions, and to explore texts in the company of other readers and writers. Key to the literacies contained in the standards is the accomplishment of the students' own literacy purposes (IRA/NCTE, 1996). The chapters of this book mirror the broad conception of texts and literacies advocated by the ELA standards. We believe that adherence to these standards, facilitated through collaboration between the content-area literacy specialist and the ELA teacher, will prepare students to face the complex literacy tasks of the 21st century. The following vignette illustrates the results of such collaboration.

Vignette: In preparation for the upcoming school year, Mrs. Costello, an 8th-grade ELA teacher, meets with Ms. Isaksen, a literacy specialist. They discuss the state standards, identify units of study that incorporate multiple genres of texts, discuss literacy strategies that would benefit the students, and decide on a theme for the school year: "How can we personally create a community that honors all individuals?" Mrs. Costello explains that in former years English has been a challenge for many of her non-native students, and certain aspects of reading have been difficult for all of her students. She expects it to be the same during the upcoming year. As they begin to discuss the details of the units, Mrs. Costello express-es a strong desire to have students read Harper Lee's classic, *To Kill a Mockingbird* (1960/2002). She is hopeful that she can make it come alive for them. She expresses some frustration with the students' response to the novel last year. As the conversations continue, the two teachers begin to realize that the students might not relate to Lee's novel as they do to a recently published novel, *Mississippi Trial, 1955* (Crowe, 2003)—a novel, unlike Lee's, written with an adolescent audience in mind. Eventually, Mrs. Costello decides to use Crowe's novel along with excerpts from Lee's nov-el to help students access themes present in both novels—themes such as getting along with parents, standing up for what is right in the face of op-position and personal risk, and understanding the complexity of humans having good and bad attributes. Additionally, Mrs. Costello determines that she will couch the reading of these novels within a unit on the Civil Rights Movement, pulling in photographs, music, video footage, and docu-ments available on the Library of Congress' website and through other Internet and traditional media.

Mrs. Costello and Ms. Isaksen also discuss literacy instruction that could be included in the unit. They realize that 8th-grade students have a hyper-sensitivity to unfairness. Life, for 8th graders, is not fair. The teachers feel like the students will have strong emotional reactions to the unfairness present in the novels and the other texts related to civil rights. They de-termine that this unit would provide a context for teaching students about building text-to-text, text-to-world, and especially text-to-self connections (Tovani, 2000).

Months later Ms. Isaksen observes Mrs. Costello's classroom during the Civil Rights unit. The class has just finished reading the novel *Mississippi Trial, 1955* and is discussing the events leading to the Civil Rights Movement. To stimulate discussion, Mrs. Costello has students follow along with the lyrics as Bob Dylan rumbles his way through "The Death of Emmett Till" (1963). She reminds the class that good readers make connections as they interact with written or oral texts. She leads the class in a brief discussion of the similarities and differences between the novel and Dylan's song. She then expands the discussion by asking students to draw connections between these texts, the website, and the excerpts from *To Kill a Mockingbird* that students have read in class. A rich discussion ensues as students point out similarities and differences between the texts.

"In addition to text-to-text connections, good readers make text-to-self connections," Mrs. Costello transitions. She then proceeds into the lesson of why some people refused to testify at the trial of Emmett Till. She connects the story to her students by asking: "Do you know anyone who might be prejudiced toward you?" and "Have any of you ever been dealt with unjustly?" Nods of agreement join raised hands as students eagerly share a few experiences. Gabe relates, "Once when I went into the store a clerk followed me the whole time I was there. She didn't say anything, but I knew she was following me because I was a Hispanic kid." Mrs. Costello follows up with the more difficult question that causes introspection: "Have you ever treated others unfairly because you were or are prejudiced?" The classroom becomes very quiet. Mrs. Costello asks students to take a few minutes to formulate their ideas in a written response and then calls on a few volunteers to begin a new discussion. Jennifer begins, "It is hard for me to admit this but . . ." It quickly becomes clear to Ms. Isaksen that even the resistant readers have engaged with the novel, deeply connecting with this story of racism and prejudice. She observes that students are eager to express their personal opinions and connections to this novel.

As part of the discussion, Mrs. Costello reads passages from the novel, pausing to model the beauty of language and to express the sheer joy of reading. She thinks aloud to show how proficient readers connect to powerful images, such as R.C.'s (a character from the novel) comment, "I swear, Hiram, I felt like all the hate I'd ever had was pourin' out of me right on to him" (Crowe, 2003, p. 199), as he recounts beating up his father. "What does he mean, is he never going back?" Mrs. Costello whispers. "I wonder if he will leave his sister Naomi there." As she asks questions and clarifies the meaning of difficult passages, she demonstrates deep engagement with text. Her students are no longer indifferent but emulate literate learners as they read and become indignant about the issues that they unearth. Amy cries out, "I can't believe he'd do that to his Pa!"

A few days later, Tanner expresses disappointment when the Civil Rights unit ends. "I was just starting to like talking about this stuff," he reports. But Mrs. Costello is thrilled when she notices that several students bring copies of *To Kill a Mockingbird* to read during the schoolwide independent reading time.

IMPROVING LITERACY INSTRUCTION THROUGH COLLABORATION

The purpose of this chapter is to provide literacy specialists with ideas that can be used to improve literacy instruction in English language arts classrooms. We categorize these improvements into three areas that correspond loosely to a literacy specialist's work with teachers of mastery classrooms, cultural heritage classrooms, and process classrooms. We suggest the following reforms: (a) a shift in instructional focus from the mastery of skills to the development of highly proficient strategic learners; (b) a broadening of the English curriculum to embrace the richness of written, spoken, and visual language; and (c) a focus on the literacies relevant to adolescents' lives.

From Skill Mastery to Strategic Proficiency

Our proposal of a shift in instructional focus from the mastery of skills to the development of highly proficient strategic learners requires some clarification of the constructs we use. "Skills" refer to automatic processes literate individuals use as they construct meaning with a text (Paris, Wasik, & Turner, 1991). "Strategies," in this context, refer to heuristics proficient readers willfully and consciously use in order to improve their comprehension of a text. One additional clarification about the construct of strategies is needed. As we discuss strategies in this chapter, we refer to cognitive comprehension strategies that readers use rather than instructional strategies that teachers use. In reference to the latter, we use the term *activities* or *methods*. Implicit in this definition of strategies is the notion of metacognition, the ability to monitor one's comprehension, notice comprehension breakdowns, and employ some measure to address the problem. Research on comprehension promotes the use of many strategies, but seven have emerged across studies: activating background knowledge, questioning, making inferences, determining importance, employing fix-up strategies, visualization, and synthesizing or making connections.

Proficient readers use three types of knowledge of strategies, according to Paris, Lipson, and Wixson (1983): (1) declarative knowledge (what is it?), (2) functional knowledge (how will I use it?), and (3) generative knowledge (when will I use it?); the third component allows a transfer of English-specific strategies and knowledge into new situations beyond the classroom, and into "real life" (Grierson, 2006).

The vignette illustrates overt strategy instruction. Before the unit begins, Mrs. Costello and Ms. Isaksen identify a strategy—making connections—that they believe will help students negotiate the texts of the Civil Rights unit. In teaching the unit, Mrs. Costello discusses the strategy openly with her students, models the strategy, and gives them multiple opportunities to use the strategy. Mrs. Costello helps students practice making connections by bringing in texts that are directly related to the novel. Additionally, she asks questions intended to build text-to-self connections. Mrs. Costello builds similar lessons on other literacy strategies that are appropriate to the specific texts being used throughout the school year. She is trying to build highly proficient strategic readers.

It should be noted that Mrs. Costello and Ms. Isaksen acknowledge the need for students to be strategic readers as they examine texts of *all* genres. Mastery of English strategies include the receptive modes of reading, viewing, and listening, as well as the expressive modes of writing, speaking, and performing. Students in Mrs. Costello's classroom are given support as they engage in personal writing and discussions of personal and sensitive issues. Additionally, Mrs. Costello's students have opportunities to work with the print and visual texts of the Internet. She and Ms. Isaksen have explored the standards, finding that they extend to technology-related strategic literacy learning—a new and somewhat frightening territory. English teachers are expected to help students negotiate the increasing hybridity and intertextuality that are apparent in digital texts. Literacy specialists who develop expertise in these 21st-century literacies can assist English teachers in this effort.

Ms. Isaksen served an important role in the development of strategy instruction in Mrs. Costello's class. She helped Mrs. Costello create a list of strategies appropriate for instruction with the novel. She discussed with Mrs. Costello the importance of students learning to make connections. We believe that literacy specialists like Ms. Isaksen can help improve the strategy instruction taking place in ELA classrooms. Further, we believe that teachers of mastery-focused classrooms, with gentle prompting by literacy specialists, can be induced to shift the focus of their instruction from skill development to the development of literacy strategies that adolescents willfully employ to improve their interactions with a wide variety of texts.

Broadening the English Curriculum

In the vignette above, the curriculum for the year is built around an overarching question or theme, "How can we personally create a community that honors all individuals?" Mrs. Costello has used this universal question, with Ms. Isaksen's help, to choose a variety of print and nonprint, traditional and nontraditional texts that will help her students make sense of their world. These texts include informational texts, historical primary source documents, historical photographs, music, song lyrics, and historical video footage available online. Of course, at the center of the students' literacy activities is a novel, a traditional text of ELA classrooms. This novel, however, has been carefully selected to meet the needs of Mrs. Costello's students. It tells a story rich in adolescent relationships, problems, and decision making. Students read about young people their age making life-and-death decisions about friends, struggling to get along with their parents, recognizing that their heroes have serious character flaws, facing discrimination, and learning to get along with people from cultures that are different from their own—all issues that Mrs. Costello knows the students in her class have experienced.

What role does the traditional canon play in Mrs. Costello's classroom? She recognizes that one purpose of public education is to expose students to important texts that form a foundation of American culture and democracy. The world is full of allusions to Shakespeare, Brontë, and Fitzgerald, and she wants her students to understand the world. Additionally, these classics introduce human themes that are universal in scope and experience. She wants all students, not just those in the honors classes, to know and appreciate these classic works. On the other hand, she knows that forcing the classics on disinterested adolescents does little to enhance their literacies. Students who struggle to engage with great literature, particularly in the absence of literacy instruction, are unlikely to consider the universal themes or to enjoy the language that draws ELA teachers to those classics. Mrs. Costello, with the help of Ms. Isaksen, reached a difficult compromise in planning her Civil Rights unit. Students were introduced to the classic *To Kill a Mockingbird* by reading carefully selected excerpts. They met Atticus Finch. They were exposed to the beauty of the language in Lee's novel. And, most important, they explored the themes of the novel that will help them know how to be better human beings. But the focus of the unit was not merely on the novel. Instead, students used the novel within the context of a wider unit of study and in conjunction with other texts of a variety of genres.

Embracing multiple new descriptions of text and genre can be extremely freeing in one sense, but without support from knowledgeable peers such as Ms. Isaksen, it also can create anxiety for ELA teachers. When competing literacy models muddy the boundaries of the English curriculum, deciding what is worthwhile to examine and teach in the classroom becomes problematic. With the roadmap of the ELA standards in place, and the help of literacy specialists like Ms. Isaksen, teachers can define what a comprehensive curriculum framework could look like, including what is essential to learn and know, how to communicate English thinking and knowledge, and how English literacy fits into a social context. In Mrs. Costello's ELA classroom, she now helps her students to understand a broadened notion of literacy as they "peel off layer after layer of concerns brought to bear—social, biographical, historical, linguistic, textual—and at the center [they] find the inescapable transactional events between readers and texts" (Rosenblatt, 1978, p. 175).

Literacies Relevant to Adolescents' Lives

Much has been written about building a bridge between adolescents' out-of-school literacies and the academic literacies we want students to develop in schools. Mastery model instruction gathers the materials to build the bridge. Cultural heritage instruction gives adolescents a glimpse of the other side. Certainly, resources and vision are essential, but they are not enough. The vignette presents several elements in the process of building the bridge and persuading adolescents to cross. Students need to be able to access texts if they are to engage deeply with them. Overt strategy instruction is one way ELA teachers can help students become more proficient readers, but it is only one element of effective ELA instruction. Students need motivation to engage with texts. ELA teachers must choose carefully the texts that they will use in their classrooms; they must offer texts with which adolescents connect. But above all, ELA teachers must give students opportunities to engage in powerful and authentic ways with language in its written, spoken, and visual media. The vignette shows students reading, writing, and speaking with great passion about important topics that are directly related to their lives. And, ultimately, we hope the students in Mrs. Costello's classroom will find a way to create a community that honors all individuals, as the year's theme suggests.

CHAPTER SUMMARY

Literacy specialists can be a valuable resource to ELA teachers as they address the changing face of ELA education. Because English is traditionally a print-focused discipline, some English teachers, especially those from mastery and cultural heritage models, may have had little formal training in teaching literacy as defined in this book. Research on adolescent literacy and content-area literacy provides practical suggestions for secondary teachers. Literacy specialists should familiarize themselves with this research and help ELA teachers apply it in their classrooms. The gradual reform that is taking place has come about with the ELA standards and the realization that English teachers need to address the literacy-specific needs of a formerly ignored population—adolescents who lack reading proficiency. Bringing a heightened adolescent literacy focus into English classrooms, however, has opened a proverbial can of worms, as Lee and Spratley (2010) remind us: "Wrestling with the tensions of addressing content standards and helping students learn to read better is complex and requires a principled and systematic approach to text selection, sequencing, and coordination with other discipline-related problem solving" (p. 16).

Without the help of a dedicated and seasoned literacy specialist, the broad and balanced view of literacy that Crowe endorses in the beginning of this chapter might be lacking in Mrs. Costello's classroom, despite her best efforts. The rich experiences that we instead find in the vignette above are due to the collaborative efforts of an open-minded teacher and a literacy specialist who offers practical assistance on how to prioritize, integrate, and best manage the complex demands of teaching English to improve adolescents' lives.

REFERENCES

Bostwick, P. (1935). Achievement in language arts in the secondary schools. *The English Journal, 34*(3), 161–167.

Campbell, L., Eichacker, N., Tousignant, C., Ricci, G., Woodward, D., Levine, M., & Hamilton, K. (2003). *African-American odyssey: A quest for full citizenship*. Retrieved December 11, 2009, from http://memory.loc.gov/ammem/aaohtml/exhibit/aointro.html

Crowe, C. (2003). *Mississippi trial, 1955*. New York: Penguin.

Dylan, B. (1963). *The death of Emmett Till* [Special rider music]. Retrieved November 14, 2009, from http://www.bobdylan.com/#/songs/death-emmett-till

Grierson, S. (2006). Preparing for workplace literacy or "real life" through content area instruction. *English Leadership Quarterly, 28*(3), 6–8.

Grierson, S., Thursby, J., Dean, D., & Crowe, C. (2007). *Mississippi trial, 1955*: Tangling with text through reading, writing, and discussion. *English Journal, 96*(3), 80–85.

Hirsch, E. D. (1987). *Cultural literacy: What every American needs to know*. Boston: Houghton Mifflin.

IRA/NCTE. (1996). *Standards for the English language arts*. Newark, DE: International Reading Association.

Lee, C. D., & Spratley, A. (2010). *Reading in the disciplines: The challenge of adolescent literacy. A final report from Carnegie Corporation of New York's Council on Advancing Adolescent Literacy*. New York: Carnegie Corporation.

Lee, H. (2002). *To kill a mockingbird*. New York: HarperCollins. (Original work published 1960)

National Council of Teachers of English/International Reading Association. (1998). *Standards for the English language arts*. Urbana, IL: Author.

Paris, S. G., Lipson, M. Y., & Wixson, K. K. (1983). Becoming a strategic reader. *Contemporary Educational Psychology, 8*, 293–316.

Paris, S. G., Wasik, B. A., & Turner, J. C. (1991). The development of strategic readers. In R. Barr, L. Kamil, P. B. Mosenthal, & P. D. Pearson (Eds.), *Handbook of reading research* (Vol. 2, pp. 815–860). New York: Longman.

Peters, C. W., & Wixson, K. K. (2003). Unifying the domain of K–12 English language arts curriculum. In J. Flood, D. Lapp, J. R. Squire, & J. M. Jensen (Eds.), *Handbook of research on teaching the English language arts* (pp. 573–589). Mahwah, NJ: Erlbaum.

Rosenblatt, L. (1978). *The reader, the text, the poem: The transactional theory of the literary work*. Carbondale: Southern Illinois University Press.

Tovani, C. (2000). *I read it but I don't get it: Comprehension strategies for adolescent readers*. Portland, ME: Stenhouse.

CHAPTER 9

(Re)Imagining Literacies for Science Classrooms

Roni Jo Draper

Marta Adair

Societies face numerous pressing problems—problems associated with securing safe food supplies, reducing carbon emissions, protecting endangered wildlife, and developing new medicines. Solving these problems and many others requires individuals with an understanding of science and scientific processes. It also requires an informed public that is able to consider policy positions and make informed decisions. These scientists and citizens require an education in science that allows them to understand and critically evaluate scientific arguments. This is at the heart of scientific literacy.

Reform documents (National Research Council, 1996, 2000) have outlined an agenda for science education to promote scientific literacy for all—future scientists and nonscientists alike. Although the term *scientific literacy* is used, it generally has been applied by science educators to describe knowledgeability of science content and the processes used to develop, test, and critique scientific theories. This knowledgeability refers to the knowledge and skills needed both to understand science and to engage in scientific activity (e.g., discover science). While some science educators have suggested that scientific literacy be reconceptualized to include aspects of fundamental literacy or the ability to read and write the texts used to participate in scientific activities and conversations (Norris & Phillips, 2003), this notion of scientific literacy has not gained wide acceptance within the science education community. Rather, science educators have valued hands-on activities that promote inquiry, with some even suggesting that understanding science can be accomplished without reading and writing (Draper, 2002).

A handful of science educators, however, have recognized the importance of print literacy for engaging in scientific activities. For example, Lemke (2004) has described the range of texts and literacies required to participate fully in scientific activities and advocates that science teachers support those literacies. Moreover, Lemke explains that science texts are hybrid in nature in that they consist of words and other forms of representations like mathematical equations, graphs, and diagrams. Thus, he, like others (Hand, Norton-Meier, Staker, & Bintz, 2009; Yore, 2004), supports literacy instruction in science classrooms as an integral part of helping adolescents understand science. However, that literacy instruction must be consistent with the nature of science and the hybrid texts used to describe science. Lemke contends that practicing scientists must be able to negotiate and create these hybrid texts as they investigate, explain, and critique scientific concepts and processes.

In keeping with the definitions of text and literacy promoted by this book, we would expand Lemke's list of texts beyond print texts that include graphs, equations, and diagrams to include scientific apparatuses like three-beam balances and graduated cylinders, natural phenomena like riverbanks and plant cells, models that represent scientific phenomena, and oral presentations and discussions. Indeed, we would regard as important science texts any of those objects that are imbued with meaning or used to make or negotiate meaning. Therefore, the ability to negotiate and create the full range of science texts is required in order to participate fully in scientific activities, to demonstrate an understanding of the nature and content of science, and, thus, to achieve scientific literacy.

Despite the admission on the part of many science educators that print literacy is an essential aspect of scientific literacy, there remains fear that individuals working from a traditional literacy or language arts perspective will not fully grasp what science educators mean by *scientific literacy*. Rather than promoting students' knowledge of and ability to participate in science, science educators fear that literacy specialists instead will promote activities with traditional print text that actually undermine students' development of scientific literacy, such as having students read books *about science* instead of having students actually *do science*. As Yager (2004) put it, "To support reading and language arts literacy activities that violate the very essence of scientific literacy will not serve the interests of students or teachers interested in fostering the development of scientific thinking and understanding" (p. 96). The purpose of this chapter is to offer a description of instruction for science classrooms that allows adolescents to achieve scientific literacy that includes understanding scientific content, the ability to engage in scientific inquiry, and facility with scientific texts.

We begin with a description of instruction for science classrooms that honors important science content and processes. We do this in accordance with our desire to create classroom instruction that reflects disciplinary norms and practices. This instruction also provides an ideal context for the use and creation of authentic scientific texts. Next, we describe how literacy instruction that strengthens science understanding can be integrated into science classrooms and lead to scientific literacy, conceptualized as knowledge of the content, the ability to engage in inquiry, and an understanding of the nature of the texts and literacies that learners and doers of science use throughout the various phases of the inquiry process. We do this because we believe that scientific literacy cannot be achieved if adolescents cannot negotiate and create the various texts associated with scientific inquiry. Finally, we end the chapter with a discussion of how, with the assistance of literacy specialists, science teachers can locate the texts, literacies, and ultimately the instruction needed to support adolescents' development of those literacies. Ultimately, we believe that if literacy specialists have a vision of science instruction that honors inquiry, they will be in a position to help science teachers assist their students in achieving scientific literacy.

INSTRUCTION THAT HONORS CONTENT AND PROCESS

Science educators recommend that students *learn* science in a way that closely matches the way scientists *do* science. To this end, they advocate that science teachers create classrooms that engage students in inquiry. This, they suggest, allows students to simultaneously learn science content and gain the abilities associated with participating in discovering science. In this way, adolescents can come to realize that science is a human endeavor that seeks to make sense of the physical and natural world, and, ultimately, can discover for themselves the nature of science.

The National Science Education Standards (National Research Council, 2000) outline the abilities associated with inquiry that adolescents should develop. These inquiry abilities include, but are not limited to, the following: identifying questions that can be answered through scientific investigations; designing and conducting scientific investigations; using appropriate tools and techniques to gather, analyze, and interpret data; creating descriptions, explanations, predictions, and models using evidence; and recognizing and evaluating alternative explanations, predictions, and models. Individuals acquire these abilities by engaging in activities in which the abilities are required; indeed, these skills are developed in use. Moreover, these activities are mediated by texts—texts that must be read and written. Thus, instruction designed to promote scientific literacy must not focus simply on scientific "facts," but must also engage students in activities that invite them to question, observe, explain, and critique.

Science educators have recommended that instruction based on the 5E Learning Cycle offers one way to promote inquiry in science classrooms. Proponents of the 5E Learning Cycle suggest that learners move through five phases—*engagement, exploration, explanation, extension*, and *evaluation*—in order to both learn science and experience the process by which scientists develop, test, and confirm scientific theories (for a description of the history of the 5E Learning Cycle model and its use in science classrooms, see Bybee et al., 2006). We prefer to think of the cycle as moving through phases of engagement, exploration, explanation, and extension, with evaluation occurring at every phase (see Figure 9.1).

In the following vignette, Mr. Bhakta, the science teacher, planned a unit of instruction about heredity in collaboration with Ms. Pilsner, the literacy specialist. Mr. Bhakta was committed to using the 5E Learning Cycle as a model for guiding his instruction. Ms. Pilsner was committed to helping Mr. Bhakta identify the important texts and literacies needed for students to participate fully in the unit. They recognized that the scientific concepts related to heredity are difficult to investigate in a science classroom because examining genetic traits passed on to offspring from parent organisms requires the observation of an organism through a reproductive cycle and a life cycle. Despite the few authentic activities appropriate for classrooms related to heredity (e.g., work with fruit flies and mealworms), Mr. Bhakta and Ms.

FIGURE **9.1.** 5E Learning Cycle Model

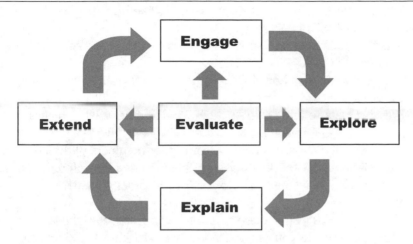

Pilsner were able to plan a unit to engage the students in inquiry that required them to practice the skills associated with inquiry as they learned content.

Mr. Bhakta opens his 7th-grade unit on heredity by having pairs of students draw slips of paper from a beaker. Each slip of paper has a pair of organisms written on it. Once all the students have their organism pairs, he tells them that they will act as curators of an organism museum.

"You and your partner will create an exhibit for the museum in which you will compare and contrast the two organisms you have just drawn from the beaker," he explains. "Your exhibits must fit on top of two desks," he continues, "and the museum will open in 3 weeks. The visitors to the museum will be the entire 5th grade of Meadow Park Elementary School." The organism pairs that Mr. Bhakta created consist of organisms that are closely related, such as black bears and polar bears, moths and butterflies, and trout and salmon.

"What sort of things do you need to know about your organisms in order to create your exhibit?" asks Mr. Bhakta during this part of the unit, designed to engage the students. "Make a list with your partner." Students begin brainstorming with their partners and making lists. After a few minutes, Mr. Bhakta brings the class together and begins making a class list on the board.

"We need to find out where they live," offers one student.

"We need to find out about their life cycle, like how they are born and how long they live," offers another.

"What are their characteristics? Like, what do they look like, how big are they, that kind of stuff."

"We need to find out how the two organisms are alike if we are going to make a display about them together."

"We also have to find out how they are different or what makes them special."

After recording a few more ideas from other members of the class, Mr. Bhakta points out to the class that they have made an impressive list. At this point the students are ready to explore in order to learn about their organisms.

"As we are investigating these pairs of organisms, be on the lookout for how the places where you can find them are related to the characteristics that allow them to be successful in those places," suggests Mr. Bhakta. "We also have to make a plan for how we are going to find all of this out."

Once the students devise a plan for their inquiries, they spend the next 2 weeks searching the Internet, books, and magazines to find out all they can about their organisms, the places they live, and how they live in those places. Mr. Bhakta also has arranged for a visit by a local wildlife biologist to speak to the students about local organisms and the local habitat that supports them.

Each day of the unit Mr. Bhakta guides the students through mini-inquiries designed to help them understand concepts related to natural selection and how genetic traits of surviving organisms are passed to offspring. These mini-inquiries allow students to gain access to explanations for scientific concepts and to extend those explanations to their own organism pairs, like the day students engaged in a simulated investigation of birds' beaks.

Mr. Bhakta begins the inquiry by explaining, "We are going to use models to investigate how different birds use their beaks to obtain food." Each pair of students has a packet that includes images of birds, a list of food sources (aquatic plants, insects on the surface of the ground, insects underground or in a hollow tree, fish, worms, and nectar), and an inventory of resources available in the lab (toothpicks, egg cartons, straws, boxes of cereal, tweezers, gummy worms, graduated cylinders, spoons, chopsticks, Styrofoam, and a variety of small candies).

"Look through your packets and devise a way to model the beaks and the food sources, given the materials available to you in the lab. Then, with your group, come up with questions that you can test, given the materials available to you."

The students return to their groups and begin discussing and recording their ideas. After a few minutes Mr. Bhakta brings the class back together and leads a discussion about how the class can model the beaks and the food sources.

"Let's hear some questions you think we can test with the materials we have here," says Mr. Bhakta.

"Can we match the beak to the food source?" asks one student. Mr. Bhakta records the question on the board and signals for more questions.

"Is there a bird beak that is better at getting food than other beaks?" asks another student.

While Mr. Bhakta records the question, he asks, "What do you mean by 'better'?"

Another student from the same group quips, "Like maybe there are beaks that can get food from more than one food source."

Mr. Bhakta continues to record questions on the board and, with some discussion from the class, puts a star next to the best testable questions. "Now, choose one of the starred questions and devise a plan to test your question."

Students return to their groups. The room buzzes with students making plans. Mr. Bhakta moves through the room, checking plans and posing questions to groups about their plans.

Once groups have their plans approved, they gather materials and begin testing beaks against the food sources. Mr. Bhakta continues his close monitoring of the groups and guides them to keep careful records of their investigations. Mr. Bhakta ends the inquiry by having students use their data to answer their questions and share their answers with the rest of the class.

"Based on the inquiries we've conducted, we have some insights about how the specialized structures of organisms give them advantages in their environments."

Finally, the students turn to the books and articles they have gathered about their organism pairs. They use the information in the various texts to complete a matrix like the one in Figure 9.2.

In the vignette, Mr. Bhakta moved students through the 5E Learning Cycle. First, he organized the entire unit as an ongoing inquiry in which the students learned about their pair of organisms. He *engaged* them by providing them with a task, the creation of an

FIGURE 9.2. Specialized Structure Matrix

Specialized Structure Matrix for _____ & _____

Organism	Where in the world can it be found?	What is the climate of the environment?	What other kinds of organisms live in the environment?	What specialized structures help it to survive in the environment?

organism museum, which provided a context for students to generate questions about their organisms. They then *explored* various texts and participated in activities in order to learn about organisms in general and their organisms in particular. Next, they heard *explanations* from Mr. Bhakta about heredity, specialized structures, and environments. Finally, they *extended* their understandings of the central concepts of the unit to their own organism pairs and used that information to create an exhibit appropriate for 5th-grade students.

    Mr. Bhakta provided instruction that allowed students access to important scientific ideas and enabled them to experience the kind of questioning and investigating done by scientists. In fact, they were able to access scientific ideas through the variety of texts available to them throughout the unit, making scientific literacy a possibility for all students. For example, the work of creating exhibits comparing two organisms forced students to examine the specialized structures of the organisms and how those structures gave the organisms an advantage in their particular environments. Moreover, they were able to create and use texts in ways that allowed them to participate fully in scientific investigation, explanation, and communication. For example, students learned to pose questions, record and manipulate data, make inferences based on data, and make scientific explanations based on available evidence.

Prior to the implementation of the unit, Mr. Bhakta and Ms. Pilsner collaborated to design instruction that would promote science literacy. Ms. Pilsner offered ideas for helping students organize their thinking in preparation for creating their museum exhibits. She also helped locate some source material students used to gather information about their organisms, taking care that the texts she suggested were consistent with scientific discourse. However, her greatest contribution was the suggestion to use matrices to help students organize information and articulate the similarities and differences between organisms and environments. She understood that if literacy specialists who work with science teachers do not honor the nature of knowledge and knowledge production in science settings (adopt inquiry instructional methods), they run the risk of making recommendations to science teachers that can undermine the achievement of scientific literacy. Moreover, she understood that she must work to help design instruction that actually allows students to acquire the literacies associated with the full range of science texts.

INTEGRATING LITERACY INSTRUCTION IN SCIENCE CLASSROOMS

Literacy instruction for science classrooms should not lead to a different kind of science instruction, but should enhance instruction in a way that leads to improved scientific understanding and enhanced capacity to participate in science. New texts need not be introduced in the name of literacy instruction because adolescents confront a wide variety of texts as they move through the 5E Learning Cycle (see Figure 9.3 for examples of some of the texts and literacies that learners of science confront). Moreover, the abilities associated with inquiry (e.g., questioning, predicting, describing, explaining, modeling, defending, and communicating) require the literacies needed for learning and doing science. Thus, science teachers must support adolescents as they develop these literacies as a regular part of science instruction.

FIGURE 9.3. Texts and Literacies Associated with the 5E Model of Science Instruction

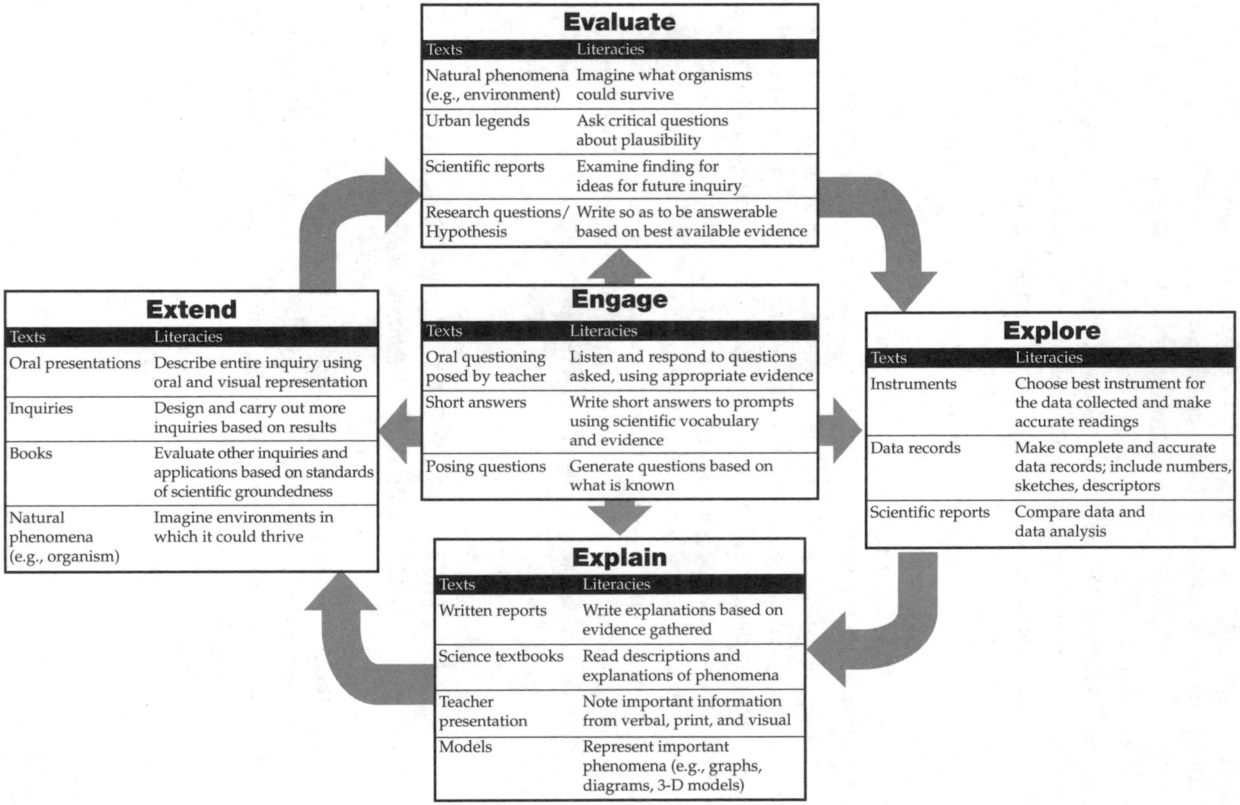

Evaluate

Texts	Literacies
Natural phenomena (e.g., environment)	Imagine what organisms could survive
Urban legends	Ask critical questions about plausibility
Scientific reports	Examine finding for ideas for future inquiry
Research questions/ Hypothesis	Write so as to be answerable based on best available evidence

Explore

Texts	Literacies
Instruments	Choose best instrument for the data collected and make accurate readings
Data records	Make complete and accurate data records; include numbers, sketches, descriptors
Scientific reports	Compare data and data analysis

Engage

Texts	Literacies
Oral questioning posed by teacher	Listen and respond to questions asked, using appropriate evidence
Short answers	Write short answers to prompts using scientific vocabulary and evidence
Posing questions	Generate questions based on what is known

Explain

Texts	Literacies
Written reports	Write explanations based on evidence gathered
Science textbooks	Read descriptions and explanations of phenomena
Teacher presentation	Note important information from verbal, print, and visual
Models	Represent important phenomena (e.g., graphs, diagrams, 3-D models)

Extend

Texts	Literacies
Oral presentations	Describe entire inquiry using oral and visual representation
Inquiries	Design and carry out more inquiries based on results
Books	Evaluate other inquiries and applications based on standards of scientific groundedness
Natural phenomena (e.g., organism)	Imagine environments in which it could thrive

During their planning sessions prior to the implementation of the unit, Mr. Bhakta and Ms. Pilsner designed assessment and learning activities. Ms. Pilsner helped Mr. Bhakta see that his students would confront and create a wide range of texts as they moved through the inquiry. Mr. Bhakta recognized that students would have to generate texts as they brainstormed questions, and that they would have to read information about various organisms from Internet sites. Despite the hybridity of these texts, Mr. Bhakta saw only the print components of these books, articles, and Internet sites as text. With Ms. Pilsner's help, he came to see the video, audio, maps, and other images that were part of the resources as important science texts that students must learn to read and write. Ms. Pilsner also helped Mr. Bhakta understand that the presentations he made (which included his words, visual displays, and gestures) also served as important texts as he led discussions and offered brief lectures as part of the explanation phase of the 5E Learning Cycle. With this expansion of the conception of text, he suggested that the scientific phenomena themselves were also texts that his students had to read. At first, Ms. Pilsner wondered whether this suggestion pushed the conception of text too far. However, Mr. Bhakta supported his position by pointing out that the students were expected to read scientific phenomena, or examine an organism and make inferences about the kind of environment that could support it, as well as read an environment and make inferences about the characteristics of organisms that would thrive in it. Finally, Ms. Pilsner and Mr. Bhakta made a list of the texts that students were expected to create as they worked to complete their exhibits—data tables, maps, pictures of habitats, and descriptions that compared and contrasted their pairs of organisms.

Rather than simply give students access to texts or just expect students to create a variety of texts, Mr. Bhakta and Ms. Pilsner sought to provide instruction that would enable students to get the most out of their interactions with texts. Return, for a moment, to Mr. Bhakta's classroom to see how he provided literacy instruction during his unit on heredity.

"Use the information from your completed matrix [see Figure 9.2] to create a paragraph that compares and contrasts the specialized structures of your organisms," explains Mr. Bhakta. On an overhead transparency Mr.

Bhakta displays a list of signal words for comparing and contrasting that include *similar to, different than, alike, unlike, instead, both, likewise,* and *while.* Mr. Bhakta uses these words, along with information from a completed matrix about beavers and otters, to create a sample paragraph. While he writes his paragraph on the board, he explains how to use the words found in the list of signal words to create the compare/contrast paragraph. After he models how to write the paragraph, students work with their partners and use their matrices to create their own paragraphs. Once students complete a draft of their paragraphs, they trade their paragraphs with another pair of students. The students underline the signal words and put a check next to the ones that were used correctly. Students then make a list of questions about the specialized structures that they expect to answer to while reading the paragraph. When students get their own paragraphs back, they use the peer feedback to revise their paragraphs before they are published as part of their organism exhibit.

During their planning, Ms. Pilsner suggested that Mr. Bhakta provide his students with the specialized structure matrix to help them gather information about their organisms. Indeed, the fact that students had a clear purpose for their reading allowed them to locate the most valuable information from the various resources they used. Ms. Pilsner also presented ideas for how Mr. Bhakta could provide instruction to help his students create paragraphs to compare and contrast the specialized structures of their organism pairs using the information or evidence they found from their reading. Mr. Bhakta found it convenient to use the completed matrices to support his instruction. It is clear that Mr. Bhakta was able to integrate literacy instruction within his inquiry-based science instruction in a way that did not distract from the science. On the contrary, his literacy instruction made it possible for adolescents to learn powerful science as well as acquire the skills related to discovering and doing science.

Mr. Bhakta went on to provide similar literacy instructional support for the graphs and maps that students created for their exhibits. This kind of literacy instruction, instruction that is integrated throughout the unit, is integral to helping students learn how to negotiate and create the texts associated with learning, doing, and communicating science. Moreover, it is also integral to helping students access scientific content and practice the skills associated with scientific literacy.

DESIGNING SCIENTIFIC LITERACY INSTRUCTION

Before science teachers can adequately support adolescents' acquisition of the literacies associated with learning and doing science, they must identify the texts adolescents confront in science classrooms and determine the literacies required in order to negotiate and create those texts. Thus, literacy specialists and science teachers who have worked together to do this will be in a position to collaborate to design literacy instruction around those texts and literacies. When science teachers and literacy specialists work together to locate the texts, literacies, and literacy instruction appropriate for science classrooms, they reduce the risk of introducing texts and literacies that are not appropriate for science. However, this does require considerable effort on the part of literacy specialists and science teachers, effort that is best described as a series of steps.

First, they must work together to locate texts. This can be done by studying instructional units and making a list of the texts used during all phases of instruction. These texts must include those used and created by students as they participate in learning activities (e.g., instructional videos, textbooks, measurement equipment, observational notes, discussions, organisms in a Petri dish) and those used and created during assessment activities (e.g., short answers, inquiry reports, graphs, demonstrations, interpretations based on scientific observations, models). This list would represent the texts central to success in the science classroom and, therefore, the texts with which adolescents must gain competence.

Once the texts have been identified, literacy specialists and science teachers must work together to consider the literacies needed to negotiate and create these texts. This may be a more difficult task for science teachers who are able to create and negotiate science texts without giving much attention to their own thinking as they do so. For example, throughout the unit, Mr. Bhakta wanted the students to continually connect the specialized structures and other characteristics of their organisms with the environment in which they lived. Therefore, he wanted his students to read (or view or listen to) texts describing various organisms and think about the nature of the environment that would give the organism advantages. He also wanted his students to read descriptions of various environments and imagine what kind of organisms would thrive there. This particular literacy is tied closely to the content under study and requires a particular kind of reading of organisms and environments. Ms. Pilsner helped make these literacies visible by asking Mr. Bhakta questions such as the following: What kind of thinking do you want students to do when they confront this text? and What kind of thinking is required in order to create this text? This step, in which science teachers identify the literacies associated with scientific texts, is crucial because if they are not identified, there is no way for science teachers to support them. Moreover, a literacy specialist may not be aware of the kind of thinking that should be taking place while reading and writing the various texts associated with the unit.

Once science teachers and literacy specialists have identified the texts and literacies associated with learning, reasoning, and communicating in science classrooms, they are in a position to consider how to support adolescents' acquisition of these literacies. In some cases it may be sufficient for science teachers to offer implicit instruction (see Chapter 4), in which they simply provide opportunities for students to interact with the texts in appropriate ways. Mr. Bhakta did this by providing students with the compare/contrast matrix that guided students' thinking while reading the various texts. In other cases science teachers will need to offer explicit instruction, in which they model the literacies needed to create and negotiate science texts. Mr. Bhakta did this by modeling how to use the information from the matrix to create a compare/contrast paragraph and then provided students opportunities to practice and receive feedback. Regardless of the instruction, science teachers will likely need assistance as they make these instructional decisions, and this is where literacy specialists can be of service to science teachers.

Ultimately, literacy instruction within science classrooms requires that the science teacher help learners consider the affordances and limitations of various scientific texts (Kress, 2000). For example, consider models of atoms. Frequently these models are printed in books or displayed on screens. This allows the model to be displayed easily—a clear affordance. Moreover, the visual representation makes clearer the relationship between various parts of an atom than would a written description—another affordance. However, these models as displayed are 2D representations of a 3D object. As such, a model of an atom displayed on a page or screen may convey to the reader or viewer that the various shells of the atom or the electron orbits are all on the same plane rather than in a cloud around the nucleus—clearly a limitation of the text. Adolescents must engage in investigations of the affordances and limitations of various texts as they relate to the science content and processes being represented. Return once again to Mr. Bhakta's science classroom.

"Notice what the displays look like, how they are arranged," Mr. Bhakta says as he shows the class a video he has made of a local natural history museum. "Keep track of all the different kinds of texts the curator used to share information in the museum." After viewing the video, the students make lists of texts they would like to include in their own exhibits—photos, diagrams, maps, paragraphs, and audio recordings are just a few that students discuss.

"You've noticed that the displays consist of a variety of texts. What kinds of texts would be ideal for sharing information about your organisms?" One student points out that it would be ideal to have replicas of the organisms. Another student suggests that replicas or stuffed animals would be nice in that they would show exactly what the organism looks like, but that the replica would not allow the viewer to get a sense of how the organism lives in its environment.

"Let's create a list of texts and their features that will make it possible for the visiting 5th-grade class to read and understand your organisms," Mr. Bhakta says as he begins to record ideas from the students on the board. The class uses this list as a guide while students spend the next week creating their organism displays.

Mr. Bhakta made texts themselves the objects of instruction and helped his students consider the affordances and limitations of those texts. He required multitext displays as part of the exhibits that students created about their organisms. By the time the students were ready to begin creating their exhibits, they had completed several matrices, like the one in Figure 9.2, on many facets of the organism pairs. They also had created maps and constructed tables that contained information about their organisms. In addition, they had collected pictures from the Internet and other print media, as well as made their own sketches of the organisms, comparing them for relative size and highlighting the specialized structures that allowed the organism survival advantages in its environment. By making texts the objects of instruction, Mr. Bhakta allowed students to make decisions about how to communicate ideas about their organisms.

As Mr. Bhakta's students created texts to communicate about their organisms, they had to think simultaneously about the science ideas they wanted to represent and the audience with which they wished to communicate. This is precisely the scientific thinking and text work that should be the hallmark of scientific literacy. This kind of understanding and competence cannot be achieved by focusing solely on the science concepts; it requires intentional attention to the literacy development of adolescents in science classrooms. At the same time, this kind of understanding cannot be achieved by literacy instruction alone; it requires access to important science content and process skills. Therefore, science teachers and literacy specialists have much to offer each other in making scientific literacy a real possibility for adolescent students.

CHAPTER SUMMARY

Literacy instruction in science classrooms must help students develop rich and accurate conceptions about science and help students understand the nature of science. To accomplish this, students must be supported as they confront and create the texts central to doing science. We propose that the way to accomplish this is through instruction that adheres to the tenets of inquiry and provides opportunities for students to use, examine, and critique the various texts used and created throughout the inquiry process. Indeed, there is no shortage of texts necessary for learning and doing science. Thus, literacy instruction for science classrooms does not require the introduction of texts. Instead, the challenge of literacy instruction for science classrooms is creating coherent instruction that allows students to learn science and the accompanying literacies. Collaboration between science and literacy educators allows teachers to (re)imagine both science and literacy and create instruction that provides opportunities for adolescents to become scientifically literate.

REFERENCES

Bybee, R. W., Taylor, J. A., Gardner, A., Van Scotter, P., Powell, J. C., Westbrook, A., et al. (2006). *The BSCS 5E instructional model: Origins and effectiveness.* Colorado Springs: Office of Science Education, National Institutes of Health. Retrieved September 30, 2009, from http://science.education. nih.gov/houseofreps.nsf/b82d55fa138783c2852572c9004f5566/$FILE/ Appendix%20D.pdf

Draper, R. J. (2002). Every teacher a literacy teacher? An examination of the literacy-related messages in secondary methods textbooks. *Journal of Literacy Research, 34,* 357–384.

Hand, B., Norton-Meier, L., Staker, J., & Bintz, J. (2009). *Negotiating science: The critical role of argument in student inquiry.* Portsmouth, NH: Heinemann.

Kress, G. (2000). Multimodality. In B. Cope & M. Kalantzis (Eds.), *Multiliteracies: Literacy learning and the design of social futures* (pp. 182–202). New York: Routledge.

Lemke, J. L. (2004). The literacies of science. In E. W. Saul (Ed.), *Crossing borders in literacy and science instruction: Perspectives on theory and practice* (pp. 33–47). Newark, DE: International Reading Association and National Science Teachers Association.

National Research Council. (1996). *National science education standards.* Washington, DC: National Academy Press.

National Research Council. (2000). *Inquiry and the national science education standards.* Washington, DC: National Academy Press.

Norris, S. P., & Phillips, L. M. (2003). How literacy in its fundamental sense is central to scientific literacy. *Science Education, 87*(2), 224–240.

Yager, R. E. (2004). Science is not written, but it can be written about. In E. W. Saul (Ed.), *Crossing borders in literacy and science instruction: Perspectives on theory and practice* (pp. 95–107). Newark, DE: International Reading Association.

Yore, L. D. (2004). Why do future scientists need to study the language arts? In E. W. Saul (Ed.), *Crossing borders in literacy and science instruction: Perspectives on theory and practice* (pp. 71–94). Newark, DE: International Reading Association and National Science Teachers Association.

CHAPTER 10

(Re)Imagining Literacies for Visual Arts Classrooms

Amy Petersen Jensen
Diane L. Asay
Sharon R. Gray

In the past, Alicia Greene, an art teacher who serves as the district arts coordinator for Peat County School District, avoided working with school literacy specialists because she always figured that they would want her to impose some sort of reading curriculum on the educators for whom she was responsible. She supported this stance by remembering that most conversations she had had with literacy specialists were limited to terse discussions about reading art history and other written texts. But over the past few months things have changed. She has developed a working relationship with John Peck, the district literacy specialist. The two of them have been creating a literacy presentation for all of the visual arts educators working in their district. In preparation for this meeting they have already participated in lively conversations about art and literacy. They have discussed literacy in general and also have focused specifically on identifying the visual literacies that could improve content-area instruction in visual arts classrooms across the district.

In their earlier meetings Mr. Peck articulated the value of including traditional notions of print texts and their accompanying literacies into visual arts classrooms. Mrs. Greene was able to see the value in using or modifying print literacy strategies effectively in her classroom instruction but also countered that in addition to print literacies, visual arts educators are responsible for nonprint, or visual, literacies that facilitate students' critical consumption and creative production. These literacies aid students in reading and communicating visual messages to others through visual means. To support her position she calls Mr. Peck's attention to a portion of the *Standards for Art*

Teacher Preparation (National Art Education Association [NAEA], 2009), which states that "visual arts educators develop curricula that address students' ability to respond to and interpret art content, and to create meaning through art making" (p. 1). Mr. Peck assures her that this description of visual literacy is right in line with his belief in a broad notion of texts and literacies, which include visual materials like artwork.

Because of these fruitful conversations, both educators have agreed that traditional literacy strategies should be employed in some components of visual arts courses. However, they also agree that teachers in their district need to embrace a broader conception of visual and literary texts. Because of this, both educators have set a goal to engage the teachers they support in a conversation about visual texts and the literacies that can aid those teachers in their attempts to help students critically interpret and create works of visual art. As part of the preparation for the presentation, Mr. Peck has visited Mrs. Greene's classroom frequently. Today Mrs. Greene has invited Mr. Peck back to her classroom to see how their conversations have altered the way she presents visual texts and provides students with visual literacy strategies that help them critically engage with those texts. They have agreed to meet in her classroom, where he will observe the types of literacy instruction that have grown out of their discussions.

This chapter focuses on the ways that literacy specialists can help visual arts educators to effectively engage their students with print and nonprint texts in visual arts classrooms. Initially, we talk about how literacy instruction has been discussed recently by visual arts educators. Next, we identify the modes of expression and texts that are embraced in the visual arts setting. We then describe how sense-making can occur successfully in a visual arts environment when both print and nonprint literacy strategies are used in art-viewing and art-making processes. Finally, we encourage the collaboration between art educators and literacy specialists to frame curriculum goals that will enhance content-area literacy in visual arts classrooms.

LITERACY INSTRUCTION IN THE VISUAL ARTS CLASSROOM

Literacy theorist Gunther Kress (2003) begins his book *Literacy in the New Media Age* by saying, "The world *told* is different world than the world *shown*" (p. 1, emphasis added). While Kress clearly is marking a transition in traditional literacy studies, visual art educators who study visual literacy have long agreed with Kress's decree. In fact, Duncum (2004) argues that in the past decade the field of art education has refocused its agenda to embrace a broad notion of visual *culture* rather than a narrow focus of institutionalized *art*.

Visual arts educators value visual literacy experiences in which students think about and respond to visual images created by others. Those studying visual culture recognize that contemporary visual images are not simply embodiments of social reality. Instead, they see works of art as ideological sites that often bombard student viewers with powerful discursive and sociopolitical meanings (Chung, 2005; Eisenhauer, 2006). Art educators acknowledge that "to be relevant to contemporary social practice, [they] must embrace interactions between communicative modes" (Duncum, 2004, p. 253).

Art educators also value the multiple literacies associated with creating art. Researchers studying the literacies associated with visual culture often focus on the cognitive processes that take place in the creation process (Marshall, 2007). They make direct connections between image creation and significant learning or understanding that is applicable to students' lives (Bransford, Brown, & Cocking, 2000; Gray & Malins, 2004). In addition, some scholars argue that art-making processes lead to transformative learning that allows students to rethink concepts that they have studied when contemplating others' art. They assert that the transformative activity of creation generates new understandings and new perspectives that help students make sense of other learning processes associated with education in the visual arts (Sullivan, 2005).

MODES OF EXPRESSION AND TEXTS
IN THE VISUAL ARTS CLASSROOM

Visual arts educators are responsible to help their students negotiate and create symbols, images, and visual expressions. The *Professional Standards for Visual Arts Educators* (NAEA, 1993) invite classroom teachers to do this by encouraging young people to investigate a variety of modes of expression or categories of artistic expression. These modes of expression include, but are not limited to, folk and popular arts, drawing, painting, sculpture, graphic design, architecture, film and video production, installation art, commercial art, street art, and performance art.

Teachers studying these unique modes of expression will introduce students to a variety of texts that are important to the mode of expression. For example, in a classroom where students are investigating folk art, they might encounter texts like metalwork, pottery, textiles, or quilts created in a particular culture or site. In contrast, students focusing on painting might explore still life, landscapes, portraiture, or collage as visual texts.

Good art teachers engage their students in the talk, tools, techniques, and processes inherent to each art text to help students understand and use each of these texts. In this way they are helping visual arts students to "learn vocabularies and concepts associated with various [interactions] in the visual arts" (NAEA, 1993, p. 21). For instance, a teacher introducing students to the quilted paintings of the visual artist Faith Ringgold first might explain to students ways of talking and thinking about her quilted paintings. Second, he/she might help the students identify the tools and techniques Ringgold used in the creation of the work of art. Third, the educator could provide students with opportunities to practice with the creation concepts and processes that seem inherent to Ringgold's work. Fourth, the art educator might ask students to experiment with and consider ways in which the tools and techniques present in the artist's work could inform or expand their own future practice as art-makers. Additionally, the teacher might provide a space in which students could challenge or contest the messages present in the work of art. In each of these teaching moments, art educators can introduce literacy or meaning-making opportunities that aid students in the development of art literacy.

MEANING-MAKING IN THE VISUAL ARTS CLASSROOM

Meaning-making in the visual arts classroom should occur when students and teachers are viewing (analyzing, reflecting, deconstructing) art in the classroom, at a museum, or while shopping in a public venue. With this idea in mind, visual arts teachers should introduce students to visual texts purposefully. When initiating viewing experiences with students, teachers are directed to provide students with opportunities to "think, communicate, reason, and investigate" the art object. Instructional strategies are intended to familiarize students with "ideas, concepts, issues, dilemmas, and knowledge" in order to make meaningful inferences about, or to construe meaning from, the art object (NAEA, 1993, p. 18).

Meaning-making also should occur when teachers and students are creating art. The educator prompting student art-making also wants students to "think, communicate, reason, and investigate" as they participate in art-making processes and engage in experimentation with the qualities and techniques associated with producing a particular work of art (NAEA, 1993, p. 21). For example, students and teachers might ask questions about the art object, such as: Why was this particular work selected? Who selected the artwork? For whom was the artwork created? For what purposes was it created? To this end, the *Professional Standards for Visual Arts Educators* (NAEA, 1993) state that students should "understand the relationships among art forms and between their own work and [the critical investigation] of others . . . [and] have a broad and in-depth understanding of the meaning and import of the visual world in which they live" (p. 21).

COLLABORATION BETWEEN THE LITERACY SPECIALIST AND THE VISUAL ARTS EDUCATOR

In collaboration, the literacy specialist and the visual arts educator can identify curriculum goals that will enhance content-area instruction and literacy in the visual arts classroom. Literacy specialists seeking to aid visual arts educators in these meaning-making or literacy experiences can look for similarities between their literacy goals for content-area classrooms and the goals stated above that govern most visual arts classrooms. For example, an appropriate set of goals was set forth by Gee (2000). A literacy specialist might use Gee's goals successfully for content-area literacy instruction in conversations with art educators. These goals include situated practice, overt instruction, critical framing, and transformative knowledge. The following outline summarizes Gee's (2000) description of these goals:

1. Students have a right to situated practice, or hands-on, embodied learning experiences that involve authentic and meaningful talk, texts, tools, and technologies.

2. Students should have effective overt instruction that focuses the learners' attention on, and allows for a meta-awareness of, and reflection on, patterns and relationships in the languages and practices being taught.
3. Students should understand critical framing, or how what they are learning relates to other domains.
4. Students have the right to produce and transform knowledge, not just consume it.

Using Gee's framework (or other frameworks like it) as a tool to investigate curriculum together, the literacy specialist and the visual arts educator can work in partnership to identify the vocabularies, concepts, and contexts associated with various types of visual art forms and content-area literacy goals. Together they will be better able to help students meet the unique literacy goals of the visual arts classroom.

The earlier vignette demonstrates that through conversation, collaborative planning, and careful observation of quality teaching, content-area literacy specialists and art educators can begin to see connections between their unique literacy goals for classrooms. In the vignette we learn that Mr. Peck and Mrs. Greene have engaged in conversation about visual arts content and literacy. Together they have explored the texts and literacies that occur in her classroom. Mrs. Greene has introduced Mr. Peck to practical examples of visual literacy, and Mr. Peck has provided her with a literacy framework through which she can examine her practice and reflect on her teaching. Their collaboration benefits her instruction (as well as that of the other art educators they hope to include in future discussions).

This is evidenced in the continuation of the vignette below, in which Mr. Peck observes Mrs. Greene's visual arts classroom to see how their conversations have influenced her literacy awareness in her classroom. Her classroom is steeped in visual texts, and she now introduces her students to several visual literacies necessary to negotiate the visual culture texts they encounter both in and outside of her classroom (i.e., in public spaces, commercial spaces, cultural spaces, personal spaces, and so on). Mr. Peck's goal is to identify the ways that their collaboration has enhanced the visual arts classroom.

As Mr. Peck enters Mrs. Greene's AP art classroom, he is intrigued by what seems to be strategically placed clutter. Tables and countertops are covered with lunch boxes, CD covers, comic books, toys, clothing, advertisements from magazines, and food labels. Mrs. Greene assures him that the clutter is pertinent to the lesson and invites him into the classroom.

When class begins, Mrs. Greene asks her students to explore the objects placed around the room and to make note of what each object might represent. She also asks the students to think about the source of the object or who created it. In addition, she asks them to consider the possible messages the object might present. The students mill about the room picking up objects, sometimes holding them up or turning them over for closer investigation.

From the corner of the room Gemma laughs and then shouts, "Hey, these are my jeans!" She holds up a pair of pants that had been strewn across one of the art tables and compares its pocket design to the jeans she is wearing. "See?" she says to the girl next to her, "look at the detail." Other students note the celebrities featured in the magazine advertisements, or admire the use of line and color in the designs on the CD cover.

Observing closely, Mr. Peck notices that Mrs. Greene is using the questioning strategies that they had discussed in earlier conversations. While he often uses the same strategy to engage students in print texts, she effectively uses the strategy when engaging students in understanding the visual texts they are exploring. When the students return to their seats, Mrs. Greene says, "What you were exploring is often called visual culture by people who discuss art. Based on your previous experience with some of these objects in your own lives and the exploration of these objects in class today, what do you think the term *visual culture* might mean?"

Gemma responds, "Well, I know it has something to do with what I wear!"

Others jump in with observations like, "It must be about seeing the things around us," and "I think it has something to do with the art that goes into all of the stuff we're looking at."

Mrs. Greene interrupts the burst of responses, saying, "I love the working ideas you present. You seem to be capturing the general notion of visual culture. Like you, I believe that visual culture has something to do with the study of contemporary culture." Passing out a handout on visual culture to the students, Mrs. Greene says, "Let's check out what someone who studies visual culture has to say about it. Her name is Eilean Hooper-Greenhill and she describes visual culture as 'focusing on questions of what is made visible, who sees what, and how seeing, knowing and power are interrelated' (2000, p. 14). Let's use one of the objects we investigated at the beginning of class—say, Gemma's jeans—to work through Hooper-Greenhill's definition of visual culture. So, let's look at the jeans with Hooper-Greenhill's quote in mind. Before you speak, think about who is seeing, how they are seeing, and how what they know about the jeans gives them power. Gemma was interested in the pockets; she made that obvious to us. So what do the rest of you observe about this artifact of visual culture?"

A boy from the back row shouts out, "The stitching on the pockets and the lack of stitching anywhere else on the jeans makes the pockets seem important—the pocket must tell us something."

A small girl sitting near the front of the classroom says that she saw the same pair of jeans in a clothing store and knows that the style of stitching on the back pockets is the logo for Rock and Republic Jeans. She adds, "Those are expensive jeans."

Gemma grabs one of the magazines from her table and jumps into the conversation: "Paying for them did take my whole paycheck, but I wanted them because they are cool." Opening the magazine, she says, "Look at how many celebrities are wearing them!" The group continues the discussion, examining and commenting on many of the items that Mrs. Greene has provided the class. Mr. Peck notes that Mrs. Greene helps students to decode, or find possible meanings, in each of the objects. To do this she invites the students to ask questions like: What am I looking at? What does this visual object signify to me? What is the relationship between the visual object and its possible message? How is this message effective?

Mrs. Greene reins the group back in by reminding them that they might have enough information to determine what Hooper-Greenhill's statement means. R.J., who has been silent for most of the discussion, says, "So what she is trying to say is that the people who make things in popular visual culture are putting meaning into them on purpose, and we may or may not understand that meaning depending on the things we already know."

"That's a really great thought, R.J.," responds Mrs. Greene as she makes a transition in the lesson. "Let's use that as we begin thinking about the work of the artist Jenny Holzer. Holzer is a conceptual artist who produced most of her artwork in the 1970s. In conceptual art the concepts and ideas are often more important than the artistic concerns of the artist. Much of her work projects text-based images onto three-dimensional spaces. Her text-based work is designed to alter the viewer's thoughts about the space in which she presents the texts."

Mrs. Greene continues, "I want to show you some examples of Holzer's work," as she projects the work "For the City" (see Figure 10.1) for the students to see. Mrs. Greene continues, "As you can see, Holzer was interested in how projecting words and ideas into conventional settings might create

FIGURE **10.1.** Jenny Holzer, "For the City"

Source: Holzer (2005)

art. The projected words challenged the intended meanings that the traditional spaces held and were intended to help people see those spaces in a
different light. Her most popular works are titled Truisms. Holzer's Truisms
are a series of interesting statements carefully designed to provoke thought.
To date Holzer has publicized these Truisms on street posters and in tele-
phone booths, projected them onto buildings, and currently posts them on
a Twitter account. For example, in the work 'For the City' (2005), Holzer
projects phrases like 'We must admit there will be music despite everything'
onto the New York Public Library in Manhattan."

Showing the students several examples of Holzer's work, Mrs. Greene
engages students in a discussion. She asks them to think about why Holzer
might select the phrases she presents, and what might lead the artist to project
them in unusual settings. She also asks them to look carefully at the selected
phrases to determine possible political, social, or other reasons that the artist
might choose to create this type of art. She says, "You might think of yourself
as an art critic who was fully informed about the conventions of conceptual
artwork or the intended meanings behind the written texts she projects, and
then put yourself in the place of a general observer on the street. What would
be different about the ways you view or think about Holzer's work?"

After more discussion, Mrs. Greene remarks that it is important to note that through her work Holzer invites viewers to consider social messages that she thinks are important to express. She is interested in sharing social messages pertinent to the time of her work, producing several vests made out of brown paper bags. Mrs. Greene continues, "I am interested in you doing the same thing today—sharing pertinent social messages through a work of art. Today we are going to design 'truism' vests that you can wear in public. Your goal will be to share this media message with at least ten people." Pulling out examples that previous students have made, she says, "Essentially you will become a walking billboard projecting messages, or truisms, that you want to send to people in your world. These truisms should include statements that you are comfortable sharing with others." She points toward the completed vests and says, "Look at these examples to further understand what we are creating."

Building on their prior knowledge of collage and mixed-media techniques, Mrs. Greene asks the students to carefully consider the ways that the vest-makers used repetition of words and images to convey meaning. She also asks the students to think about what the use of multiple textures might suggest to the viewer of these vests. Finally, she asks them to list and describe the possible thought processes that might have gone into the creation of the sample vests.

When the students seem comfortable with the assignment, she sets them loose to build their vests. She moves from table to table discussing ways that their collages can best represent the meanings each student-artist intends to present. One student cuts phrases from magazines and juxtaposes those phrases with images that might contribute to the intended statement. Another student builds a vest filled with a single phrase that is consistently repeated but recurs in a variety of colors and shapes. At one point Gemma, who is trying on her vest, says, "Mrs. Greene, my vest says exactly what's on my mind. I think I could be the next Jenny Holzer!"

Mrs. Greene reminds students as they complete the vests that they need to wear the vests in the company of at least ten people and listen to their responses. She says, "I look forward to hearing what people had to say about the vests. We will discuss it at length next time!"

As the class exits Mr. Peck approaches Mrs. Greene and says, "Thanks for letting me watch today. I saw a lot of the literacy strategies that we have discussed clearly presented in today's lesson. I am really beginning to see the ways that we can share the connections we have made between visual literacy and traditional literacy with other teachers."

The vignette demonstrates that careful observation of quality content-area teaching, and thoughtful recognition of strong connections and correlations between goals in literacy instruction and content-area objectives, led Mr. Peck and Mrs. Greene to engage in powerful conversations about literacy instruction in art classrooms. This improved Mrs. Greene's literacy awareness and instruction. In similar fashion, all content-area literacy specialists and art educators can develop literacy-infused curriculum goals for the visual arts classroom. Literacy goals common to both content-area literacy specialists and art educators are uncovered as a natural product of thoughtful discussions. Collaboration of this type leads to increased student comprehension, retention, and application of both content-area knowledge and practical literacy strategies and skills that can benefit students in any environment.

To fully demonstrate the potential of this type of productive collaboration, we must imagine the possible topics that the two educators might encounter as they unpack the events that occurred in Mrs. Greene's classroom in preparation for their presentation to the Peat County School District art educators. We do this through the lens of Gee's (2000) outline for literacy instruction, which was noted earlier in the chapter and includes: situated practice, overt instruction, critical framing, and transformative knowledge.

Visual Arts Education as Situated Practice

Visual arts educators create opportunities for their students to participate in authentic situated practice when they are thinking and talking about art and when they are creating art. Literacy specialists can help art teachers create opportunities for authentic situated practice in art classrooms by initially asking the art educator to identify the visual texts, tools, and technologies present in lessons or units of instruction. If asked this question about the lesson presented in the vignette, Mrs. Greene would have identified the examples of Jenny Holzer's art and the vests students created as the visual culture objects, or texts, that her students engaged with during the class period.

With this knowledge about the texts that were important in the visual arts environment, Mr. Peck could discuss possible methods of encouraging vibrant discussions about those particular texts. He also could point out ways that Mrs. Greene had purposefully engaged students in meaningful talk in the lesson he observed. For instance, he might observe that Mrs. Greene engaged students in meaningful talk about the topic of visual culture. She did this when she provided her students with the scholar Eilean Hooper-Greenhill's definition of visual culture. Meaningful talk occurred during the discussion of the definition because she asked them to respond to Hooper-Greenhill's quote using the prior knowledge that they gleaned from exploring the visual objects. She aided the students in this discussion by identifying the visual objects as artifacts of visual culture. In this way, she invited the students to investigate the scholar's comment through the lens of their own experience with and knowledge of the visual examples she provided. In the activity and the discussion, Mrs. Greene asked her students to investigate visual texts that they regularly encountered in the real world. In this way, she used the resources available in her classroom to better prepare students to interact critically with texts they are bombarded with in their everyday lives.

Overt Instruction in the Visual Arts Classroom

Overt instruction can be effectively used in visual arts classrooms to focus students' attention on vocabulary and concepts associated with the type of artwork they are studying. In current visual arts classrooms, educators often equate overt instruction with the lectures in which teachers introduce their students to an influential time period, artist, visual text, or tool. If asked to identify moments of overt instruction in her lesson on visual culture, Mrs. Greene would point out the factual information that she shared with students about visual culture or the biographical information about the conceptual artist Jenny Holzer.

Mr. Peck could apply his general understanding of literacy processes to overt instruction by drawing Mrs. Greene's attention to the point in her lesson where she introduced students to the processes of creating the "truism" vest. In that instance, Mrs. Greene provided overt instruction by first presenting vests made by previous class members for the students to examine. Then she and the students listed and described the possible thought processes that might have gone into the creation of the sample vests. Mr. Peck might point out that in this teaching moment Mrs. Greene introduced the students to new vocabulary, directed them to key components of the vest-making process, and answered questions about their future vest creations. Mr. Peck could help her understand that through these activities she was focusing her students' attention on the vocabularies and concepts necessary to make their own vests, and thus employed literacy concepts in overt instruction.

Participating in Critical Framing

Critical framing occurs in the visual arts classroom when teachers support student learning by introducing a lens through which the students can evaluate a given text. A literacy specialist can help art educators introduce critical framing activities into their classrooms by discussing the value of perspective-taking in the visual arts setting. If asked about perspective-taking, Mrs. Greene would point out that when her students investigated art in her lesson, they assumed dual roles of viewer and creator. In the role of viewer (critic, historian, theorist, or critical consumer) they considered how others used the texts, tools, and technologies available to create the work of art. In the role of creator they considered the ways that they might employ the texts, tools, and technologies available to them to reflect on art products and processes as active cultural participants. She would assert that each role demanded different skills from the students, and that assuming both roles allowed for a more holistic development of the students.

Mr. Peck also could point to the moment in the lesson where Mrs. Greene invited the students to respond to Holzer's work as art critics who were fully informed about the conventions of three-dimensional art and as observers on the street. He might note that this kind of perspective-taking allows students to see the work of art from a variety of viewpoints. This, in turn, allows the students to practice reading the visual example from multiple positions of knowledge.

Producing and Transforming
Knowledge with Visual Arts Students

The development of strong studio skills is often central to the visual arts curriculum. This generally is accomplished through creative production experiences and hands-on learning activities. Helping students to practice with and use tools and technologies allows teachers to assess student growth and aids teachers as they help individual students improve as artists. In discussions about producing and transforming knowledge, Mrs. Greene could acknowledge that she introduced the students to the concept of visual culture. She also exposed them to the work of Jenny Holzer, a conceptual artist. Although this exposure to

Holzer did not directly involve students in creative production, Mrs. Greene also could call attention to the vest creation exercise in which students took the information they had consumed about visual culture and produced something that reflected their own understanding of and interest in the subject matter. Clearly they could transform their knowledge about visual culture into their own artistic products.

Mr. Peck might agree with Mrs. Greene that visual arts production was certainly a key component of the day's activities. He might mention that students also were required to produce and transform knowledge as they engaged with the visual objects at the beginning of the class period. He could observe that Mrs. Greene first required students to produce knowledge when they decoded the texts, or asserted possible meaning behind each text based solely on their prior knowledge of the texts. In addition, he might note that she asked them to transform that knowledge when she introduced Hooper-Greenhill's description of visual culture and asked students to unpack the quote based on their prior knowledge and exploration of the objects she provided at the beginning of class. In this way, she presented students with opportunities to produce and transform knowledge in both studio skills and critical-viewing activities.

CHAPTER SUMMARY

The collaborative effort between the art educator and the literacy specialist described in this chapter signifies a shift in thinking about the role of the literacy specialist in arts-based literacy discussions. Historically, many encounters between literacy specialists and visual arts teachers may have been limited to discussions of art history texts, as Mrs. Greene suggested at the beginning of the chapter. However, literacy specialists like Mr. Peck, who are interested in learning about visual texts and literacies, can aid visual arts educators in implementing quality visual literacy strategies in their classrooms. In addition, content-area literacy specialists who seek opportunities to learn from visual arts educators will find openings where they can introduce strategies that originally were devised to address traditional literacy to educators, some of which will aid in improved instruction and reflection on the work that happens in the visual arts classroom.

REFERENCES

Bransford, J., Brown, A., & Cocking, R. (Eds.). (2000). *How people learn: Brain, mind, experience and school.* Washington, DC: Commission on Behavioral and Social Sciences and Education, National Research Council, National Academy.

Chung, S. K. (2005). Media/visual literacy art education: Cigarette ad deconstruction. *Art Education, 58*(3), 19–24.

Duncum, P. (2004). Visual culture isn't just visual: Multiliteracy, multimodality, and meaning. *Studies in Art Education: A Journal of Issues and Research, 45*(3), 252–264.

Eisenhauer, J. (2006). Beyond bombardment: Subjectivity, visual culture, and art education. *Studies in Art Education: A Journal of Issues and Research, 47*(2), 155–169.

Gee, J. P. (2000). New people in new worlds: Networks, the new capitalism and school. In B. Cope & M. Kalantzis (Eds.), *Multiliteracies: Literacy learning and the design of social futures* (pp. 43–68). New York: Routledge.

Gray, C., & Malins, J. (2004). *Visualizing research: A guide to the research process in art and design.* Burlington, VT: Ashgate.

Holzer, J. (2005). *For the city.* Retrieved June 10, 2009, from http://en.wikipedia.org/wiki/File:Jenny_Holzer_For_the_City.jpg

Hooper-Greenhill, E. (2000). *Museums and the interpretation of visual culture.* London: Routledge.

Kress, G. (2003). *Literacy in the new media age.* London: Routledge.

Marshall, J. (2007). Image as insight: Visual images in practice-based research. *Studies in Art Education: A Journal of Issues and Research, 49*(1), 23–41.

National Art Education Association. (1993). *Professional standards for visual arts educators.* Retrieved July 13, 2009, from http://www.arteducators.org/olc/pub/NAEA/research/

National Art Education Association. (2009). *Standards for art teacher preparation.* Retrieved July 13, 2009, from http://www.arteducators.org/olc/pub/NAEA/research/

Sullivan, G. (2005). *Art practice as research: Inquiry in the visual arts.* Thousand Oaks, CA: Sage.

CHAPTER 11

(Re)Imagining Collaborations for Content-Area Literacy

Roni Jo Draper
Jeffery D. Nokes
Daniel Siebert

Many literacy educators have argued that the ways in which educators historically have thought about content-area literacy and literacy-across-the-curriculum initiatives do not address the various needs of content-area teachers and, thus, of adolescents (Draper, Hall, Smith, & Siebert, 2005; Moje, 2008; Shanahan & Shanahan, 2008; Siebert & Draper, 2008). These same literacy educators suggest that the lack of input from disciplinary experts and educators has led to underdeveloped theories of literacy for the various disciplines. Thus, content-area literacy must be (re)imagined. We believe that the work of (re)imagining must be taken up as a collaborative endeavor between literacy and content-area educators. In this chapter we focus on establishing and maintaining collaborative relationships between literacy specialists and content-area teachers so they can work together to meet the needs of adolescents.

At the beginning of this book, we noted that tensions often exist between literacy specialists and content-area teachers—tensions that make collaboration difficult. These tensions arise when literacy and content-area teachers work from narrow definitions of *text* and *literacy* and disparate sets of aims for instruction. However, we believe that this does not have to be the case. In Chapter 1 we introduced common aims and criteria that could be used to guide the design of classroom instruction that supports both literacy and content learning. In Chapter

2 we presented expanded definitions of *text* and *literacy* that account for ways of communicating, knowing, and participating within the various disciplines. To demonstrate this, authors of the content chapters presented vignettes situated in various content-area classrooms that simultaneously illustrated both (a) content-area teaching that conforms to discipline-specific teaching and learning standards, and (b) literacy instruction that addresses the literacy needs of students in particular content areas.

Authors of the content chapters have argued consistently that the (re)imagining of literacies for content-area classrooms proposed in this book not only is compatible with good content-area instruction, but in fact must be included in content-area instruction in order to meet the learning and teaching standards in the disciplines. Their (re)imagining of content-area instruction to include attention to the wide variety of texts and literacies used within the disciplines provides a compelling case for the centrality of literacy instruction in all good content-area teaching. In other words, the authors of the content chapters have demonstrated that (re)imagining content-area literacy can aid content-area teachers as they seek to achieve their content-area instructional goals.

Additionally, the glimpses into content-area classrooms presented through the vignettes found in the various content chapters can provide literacy specialists with increased insight into the nature of the disciplines. The authors have described the nature of inquiry and creativity within each discipline and, thus, the nature of the disciplinary discourse. Literacy specialists will find this information useful as they work with content-area teachers to locate the texts and literacies particular to the various disciplines. Ultimately, the authors of the content chapters also have presented, if only tacitly, descriptions of how literacy specialists might approach their work with content-area teachers.

In this chapter, we summarize across the content chapters to identify some of the common constraints under which content-area teachers work. We believe that understanding these constraints can help literacy specialists who desire to work with content-area teachers. Indeed, we argue that these constraints can be acknowledged and addressed through a (re)imagining of content-area literacy instruction. However, as we have argued throughout this book, literacy specialists and content-area teachers must work together to (re)imagine instruction that allows content-area teachers to work within these constraints and supports adolescents' continued literacy development. Therefore, after our description of the constraints faced by content teachers, we describe characteristics of collaborative relationships, followed by suggested steps that literacy specialists can take to start those collaborations. Finally, we end the chapter, and the book, with yet another invitation to readers to (re)imagine. We recognize that the (re)imagining of content-area literacy that we have shared in this book represents a mere beginning. We ask literacy specialists and content-area teachers alike to continue the conversation and work to (re)imagine content-area literacy instruction. We believe that by working together, literacy specialists and content-area teachers place themselves in the best position possible to attain what each of them care about most, namely, helping adolescents acquire the content, skills, and literacies they need to ensure their own growth and well-being, as well as contribute to the wellness of the communities to which they belong.

COMMON CONSTRAINTS
UNDER WHICH CONTENT-AREA TEACHERS WORK

Three important themes emerge from the content chapters concerning what issues must be addressed in order for a (re)imagining of content-area literacy instruction to be attractive to content-area teachers. First, a (re)imagining of content-area literacy must acknowledge that many content-area teachers feel that meeting disciplinary goals for instruction and learning requires all of their instructional time. Certainly this is true for the content-area experts who authored chapters in this book. In some disciplines, national and state standards are difficult to meet even when instructional time is used judiciously. Because of time constraints, content-area teachers may view literacy instruction that does not support disciplinary instructional and learning goals as superfluous or even somewhat detrimental. To remain relevant to content-area teachers, literacy instruction must move beyond supporting students' general reading and writing of traditional print texts and instead focus on helping students read and write the texts used to learn content and engage in disciplinary practices.

A second important theme that emerges from the content chapters is that students confront a wide range of texts that they must read and write as they learn in content-area classrooms. In the content-area chapter vignettes, these texts included shards of clay in a history class-room (Chapter 4), a pair of jeans in a visual arts classroom (Chapter 10), equations and diagrams in a mathematics classroom (Chapter 3), and design sketches in a technology classroom (Chapter 6). In each of these vignettes, students' learning in the content-area class-rooms and participation in disciplinary activities depended on their ability to read and write these texts in discipline-appropriate ways. Moreover, because of the unique nature of these texts and literacies, students depended on their content-area teachers for help in becom-ing literate with these texts. A (re)imagining of content-area literacy must acknowledge the many types of texts and literacies necessary for learning in content-area classrooms, and that students need help with those texts and literacies.

A third theme that emerges across the content-area chapters is that reform leaders in each discipline are pushing for students to learn how to engage in the practices and modes of inquiry of the disciplines. Instead of just learning *about* the disciplines, students are being encour-aged to learn how to *participate in* the disciplines. Moreover, reform leaders advocate devoting more instructional time to helping students use the perspectives and practices of the discipline to explore issues that are part of their lived worlds, and not just to investigate prob-lems that are of interest to discipline experts. This trend toward using discipline-specific modes of inquiry to address issues in the lives of adolescents is illustrated in many of the vignettes, such as the descrip-tion of a theatre teacher who helped her students acknowledge and address oppression in their lives (Chapter 7) and the description of a science teacher who guided his students in discovering how adapta-tion and evolution can help them make sense of the biological diversity in the living creatures that surround them (Chapter 9). Because disci-plinary practices and modes of inquiry have the potential to empow-er adolescents, content-area literacy should support and encourage content-area instruction that enables students to participate in authen-tic disciplinary activities.

Our (re)imagining of content-area literacy based on broad defini-tions of *text* and *literacy* can enable literacy specialists to both ease the burdens of content-area teachers and help adolescents develop mul-tiple literacies. A broadened view of text and literacy allows literacy specialists to acknowledge all of the texts that students use to learn content. Literacy specialists with a broadened perspective can work with content-area teachers to develop instructional strategies that improve students' literacy with the texts they are using to learn content. These strategies in turn can improve students' learning of content and better enable students to participate in disciplinary activities. Thus, by adopting and promoting a broadened view of text and literacy, literacy specialists place themselves in a position to directly help teachers meet content-area teaching and learning goals, support students' reading and writing of the wide variety of texts necessary to learn content, and empower students to learn content and participate in disciplinary activities. This can lead to respectful and mutually beneficial relationships between literacy specialists and content-area teachers, as we illustrate next.

CHARACTERISTICS OF COLLABORATIVE RELATIONSHIPS

In Chapter 4 the reader was introduced to Mr. Ramos, our imagined 11th-grade U.S. history teacher, who engaged students in a powerful history lesson that was intended to help them develop the sophisticated historical literacy strategies of sourcing and corroboration as they studied a variety of texts related to the Battle of New Orleans. What the reader did not see in that chapter was the collaboration between Mr. Ramos and Mr. Sampson, our imagined literacy specialist at his school, which led up to the lesson. Their interchange is narrated below.

Mr. Ramos is going to teach his 11th-grade U. S. history class about the War of 1812. He would like to engage the class in a case study on the Battle of New Orleans that occurred during that war. He knows from experience that students interact well with the song "The Battle of New Orleans" (Driftwood, 1959), made popular in 1959 by Johnny Horton. But he is uncertain how to incorporate it into a lesson. He has used the song in the past but has never been fully satisfied with the way the lesson has gone. He finds himself sitting next to Mr. Sampson, the school literacy specialist, at lunch following a faculty development meeting. During the course of their conversation Mr. Ramos mentions that he wants to use the song in his class. Mr. Sampson remembers hearing the song on the radio when he was a boy and he is very interested in how Mr. Ramos is going to use it to teach history. Mr. Ramos explains that he has been interested in using the song but has been uncertain of how to do so. They talk about a few ideas during the rest of lunch. The bell rings, marking the end of lunch and the return of students. As Mr. Ramos returns to his classroom, Mr. Sampson offers to continue the conversation after school.

That afternoon the two of them meet to discuss lesson ideas. Mr. Ramos wants to build a good lesson plan around this song. Mr. Sampson, a language arts teacher himself, is not very familiar with the battle. "What are the texts that a historian might use to study the battle?" he asks Mr. Ramos. Mr. Ramos remembers reading a letter that Andrew Jackson wrote to his commander shortly after the battle. The two do a quick search on the Internet and find this account and several other firsthand accounts of the battle and a related historical political cartoon. Mr. Sampson asks whether the students have textbooks that include an account of the battle. Mr. Ramos ensures Mr. Sampson that every U.S. history textbook describes this battle. When they look, they find that there is a description of the battle illustrated by a painting and a map showing troop movements.

Mr. Ramos, now feeling a little overwhelmed by the number of resources that he has, starts to wonder what to do with these texts. Mr. Sampson suggests that he could have different groups each study a different document and then report to the class on their document. Mr. Ramos doesn't like the idea. "That doesn't really reflect the way historians work with documents," he explains. He suggests that, instead, historians would want to do a careful analysis of all of the resources together, comparing them with one another. However, he doubts that students could engage with the texts at that level of sophistication. Mr. Sampson asks whether there is some way that the complex tasks of the historian could be simplified into basic strategies that the students could use. Mr. Ramos responds that historians always consider the source of the text. He thinks that students could be taught to pay attention to whether a source was an eyewitness, like the writer of the letter, or someone who was uninvolved in the battle, like the textbook author or the creator of the song. He thinks students also could be taught the importance of paying attention to whether the account was produced by an American or a British source.

Mr. Sampson asks more about the idea of comparing the documents that Mr. Ramos had mentioned earlier. "What if you created some type of graphic organizer that gave students a place to record the source information and then compare and contrast the content of the documents with one another? Do you think this would help students think more like historians as they engage with these texts?" Mr. Ramos agrees that a graphic organizer should help the students engage at a deeper level of reading. Together they sketch out a graphic organizer that Mr. Ramos will format the next day. Then they turn their attention to the texts that could be used in the lesson. Together they narrow down the texts that might be most appropriate, Mr. Sampson pointing out that one of the documents contains extremely challenging vocabulary that students might struggle to comprehend. They both agree that it might be too much to expect students to engage with unfamiliar content using new strategies with texts that are above the typical reading level. They rule out that text. They additionally agree that reading the political cartoon requires different literacy strategies that they don't want to include in this lesson. In the end they choose a song, a letter, a textbook account, a painting, a map, and a journal entry that students will compare.

In our (re)imagining of content-area literacy, we also envision a new relationship between content-area teachers and literacy specialists. The imagined exchange between Mr. Ramos and Mr. Sampson illustrates the type of collaboration that has been promoted throughout this book. In this collaboration, Mr. Ramos and Mr. Sampson work together to address the three constraints facing content-area teachers, namely, the demanding learning and teaching standards and goals of the discipline, the pressing literacy needs of Mr. Ramos's students as they face a wide variety of texts, and the careful positioning of students as participants in authentic disciplinary activities. An essential enabling factor of this collaboration is Mr. Sampson's broadened view of text and literacy. Mr. Sampson not only uses this perspective as he thinks about his suggestions for the lesson, but also shares this perspective with his colleague, giving Mr. Ramos a valuable alternative lens through which to view his history instruction. By combining this perspective with Mr. Ramos's understanding of the discipline of history, Mr. Sampson and Mr. Ramos are able to develop a lesson that embodies both good literacy and good history instruction.

While a broadened perspective of text and literacy is helpful in promoting beneficial relationships between literacy specialists and content-area teachers, our own experiences suggest that this perspective alone is not sufficient for creating these collaborations. In the vignette, we illustrated some of the other attributes that are essential to creating respectful, productive collaborations. While we will not provide an exhaustive discussion of the conditions necessary to sustain collaboration, we do provide a brief list of attributes that literacy specialists may find useful as they work to create and sustain collaborations that allow for a (re)imagining of content-area literacy. Our list of attributes includes approachability, humility, and open-mindedness.

Approachability

Prior to this exchange, Mr. Ramos and Mr. Sampson had developed a sense of collegiality, which facilitated their collaboration. Mr. Ramos felt secure in approaching Mr. Sampson with a question. Mr. Sampson's interest demonstrated his respect for Mr. Ramos's concern. Such collaboration requires individuals who are approachable and schools that possess a "collaborative culture" (Cornu, 2005, pp. 356-357). There must be a spirit of collegiality, mutual respect, and a desire for improvement that extends across departments to include the literacy specialist and school administrators. For example, few teachers feel comfortable intruding on another teacher's limited time. Administrators can resolve this problem by freeing up the literacy specialist's teaching schedule to allow time for meaningful interaction with content-area teachers.

Approachability is particularly important on the part of the literacy specialist. Although not explicitly stated, an implicit message of this book is that it will likely fall to the literacy specialist to initiate and foster meaningful collaborations; content-area teachers, who may not see a lot of what they do in the classroom as being related to literacy, are unlikely to initiate the conversations. Mr. Sampson must establish himself as a resource for teachers who wish to improve their instruction. The literacy specialists' appeal to content-area teachers is not what he gives them, but what they can build together. He acknowledges them as the content experts and even the literacy experts in their content area. He establishes himself as a professional and knowledgeable general literacy expert with pedagogical ideas that, when blended with a content teacher's expertise, result in improved literacy and content instruction. Becoming recognized as such a resource may take considerable time, patience, and gentleness on the part of the literacy specialist, but as relationships develop, meaningful collaboration can occur.

Humility

Both Mr. Ramos and Mr. Sampson approached the collaboration with a recognition of their own limitations and a sense of humility. Mr. Ramos admitted to Mr. Sampson that he had a literacy-related question that he could not answer. Mr. Sampson did not enter the history classroom ready to tell Mr. Ramos what to do, but admitted his ignorance when it came to the historical content, historical texts, and even historical literacies. They humbly went to work together to solve the literacy dilemma. They followed several false leads—the inclusion of texts that were inappropriate for the objectives of this lesson, for example—but they were willing to share and critique ideas until they both felt good about the results. We (re)imagine literacy specialists who view their role as one who works *with* content-area teachers to improve literacy instruction rather than working *on* content-area teachers to add literacy instruction. We also envision content-area teachers with the humility to call for help when the need arises.

Open-Mindedness

Mr. Ramos and Mr. Sampson exhibited open-mindedness in their interaction. Mr. Ramos was open to new methods of teaching, namely, the use of the graphic organizer to provide scaffolding for students who were engaging in challenging literacy practices. Additionally, Mr. Sampson welcomed the use of texts and literacies that were unfamiliar and perhaps unconventional—texts that included songs, maps, and paintings, and literacies that included sourcing and corroboration. We anticipate that content-area teachers, like literacy specialists, initially might be resistant to our expanded notion of text. However, we suggest that successful collaborations between the two will be facilitated when both accept the definitions of texts and literacies that we advocate in this book. We anticipate that such relationships will be richly rewarding for both groups of professionals. We (re)imagine content-area teachers and literacy specialists who, because of open-mindedness, continue to learn from each other.

Additionally, open-mindedness and the expanded notion of text allow teachers to include in their lessons texts that are important to students, both now and in the future. Mr. Ramos and Mr. Sampson incorporated music into the lesson, knowing that students would respond well to this popular song from the 1950s. More important, Mr. Ramos and Mr. Sampson understood that the literacy required for effective participation in society requires individuals to synthesize information from multiple, sometimes contradictory sources. Thus, they viewed this lesson as one that could help adolescents understand history while they acquired crucial skills for participating fully in the various communities to which they belong. Open-mindedness is required in order to understand the literacy demands of the 21st century and work together to prepare students to face these demands.

STEPS TO CREATING COLLABORATIONS

Once relationships have been established and content-area teachers and literacy specialists have embraced an expanded notion of text, collaborations are possible. Obviously, each interaction between literacy specialists and content-area teachers will be unique. However, the chapters of this book repeat a pattern in these interactions that should be clear to the reader. First, literacy specialists work with content-area teachers to identify the texts and literacies that are valued within a specific discipline. For example, consider the description in Chapter 10 of the way in which a literacy specialist discovered the discipline-specific texts in a visual arts classroom. In the vignette, Mr. Peck, the literacy specialist, entered the visual arts classroom well into the collaboration. However, he continued to approach his work with the visual arts teacher as a learner, not as a knower. Thus, he used his time observing Ms. Greene to learn about literacy instruction in visual arts classrooms, rather than seeking ways to teach Ms. Greene how to implement literacy activities.

Second, literacy specialists provide expertise in creating pedagogically sound literacy practices, through collaboration with the content-area teacher, that are true to the literacies of the discipline. For example, the mathematics teachers in Chapter 3 adopted a common literacy instructional strategy—K-W-L—that needed only slight modification to be useful in mathematics classrooms. That modification demonstrates the possibility of designing and implementing literacy instruction that is consistent with the discipline. However, both content-area teachers and literacy specialists must engage in honest dialogue in order to ensure that this criterion is met.

Third, literacy specialists help content-area teachers engage in disciplinary practices that connect students' classroom experiences with their worlds outside of the classroom. By doing this, educators can foster the continued development of both in-school and out-of-school literacies of adolescents. Like Mr. Ramos and Mr. Sampson in the previous vignette, literacy and content-area teachers must work together to imagine how to include popular culture texts, not simply as a way to motivate adolescents to engage in the actual texts of the discipline, but as part of the critical work of the discipline.

Several of the chapter authors have provided vignettes that demonstrate how educators might connect disciplinary practices with the lived worlds of adolescents. For example, the students in a music classroom might use their understanding of conventional music genres as they create their own music texts that conform to those genres as well as incorporate musical qualities found in Pygmy music (see Chapter 5). Likewise, popular magazines (e.g., *Popular Mechanics, Elektor Magazine*) could provide access to important content in technology classrooms while at the same time provide students opportunities to improve their print literacy skills (see Chapter 6). This is quite different from including popular texts that are only tangentially connected to the unit of study.

(RE)IMAGINING CONTENT-AREA LITERACY INSTRUCTION

In this book, we have sought to present some of our thoughts about how content-area literacy instruction might be (re)imagined to meet the needs of content-area teachers, literacy specialists, and, most important, adolescents. The purpose of sharing our (re)imagining of content-area literacy instruction, however, is not to present a finished product to be unquestioningly adopted and applied in secondary classrooms. Rather, we see our (re)imagining as simply a first step in rethinking content-area literacy. Accordingly, we intend our work to merely open up the discussion of (re)imagining content-area literacy instruction rather than serve as the defining treatise on the subject. We know that for real change to take place in secondary classrooms—change that supports adolescents' abilities to engage in disciplinary practices—literacy specialists and content-area teachers must join with us in the (re)imagining process. We believe that this (re)imagining is important work that must be done, because without it teachers are unlikely to create classrooms in which adolescents can acquire and learn powerful literacies.

These powerful literacies are those that are required to make sense of the world, examine and evaluate the status quo, and work to create a better world. Moreover, these literacies consist of both the skills and the knowledge necessary to understand, critique, and imagine a better human condition. Certainly these literacies include those used by individuals outside of school, especially the new digital literacies. These literacies also include those used to create knowledge and participate in disciplinary communities of practice, or the literacies associated with content-area learning, knowing, and communicating. Finally, in keeping with the definition offered in Chapter 2 of this book, these literacies include the content knowledge needed to negotiate and create texts in discipline-appropriate ways. Thus, understanding these literacies and creating the instruction that supports their acquisition and learning requires collaboration between literacy specialists and content-area teachers.

We believe that new classrooms must be created that allow adolescents to learn and acquire a wide range of literacies. These classrooms must be created by content-area teachers in collaboration with literacy specialists. However, these classrooms cannot be created without imagination. Just as a building cannot be built without the imagination of an architect, or a poem written without the imagination of the author, classroom instruction cannot be enacted without the imagination of teachers. As Greene (2000) has expressed, "Imagination summons up visions of a better state of things, an illumination of the deficiencies in existing situations, a connection to the education of feeling, and a part of intelligence" (p. 272). She has claimed that imagination requires an "opening of spaces for dialogue, for shared memories, for a coming together in the name of 'something to pursue'" (p. 273).

This is our desire for teachers. We invite educators, content-area teachers, and literacy specialists to open up spaces for dialogue with one another. We invite them to come together to pursue the education of adolescents. We invite them to (re)imagine content-area literacy.

Authors' note: The authors contributed equally to the authorship of this chapter.

REFERENCES

Cornu, R. L. (2005). Peer mentoring: Engaging pre-service teachers in mentoring one another. *Mentoring and Tutoring, 13*(3), 355–366.

Draper, R. J., Hall, K. M., Smith, L. K., & Siebert, D. (2005). What's more important—literacy or content? Confronting the literacy–content dualism. *Action in Teacher Education, 27*(2), 12–21.

Driftwood, J. (1959). Battle of New Orleans [Recorded by Johnny Horton]. On *American originals* [CD]. New York: Columbia. (1989).

Greene, M. (2000). Imagining futures: The public school and possibility. *Journal of Curriculum Studies, 32*(2), 267–280.

Moje, E. B. (2008). Foregrounding the disciplines in secondary literacy teaching and learning: A call for change. *Journal of Adolescent and Adult Literacy, 52,* 96–107.

Shanahan, T., & Shanahan, C. (2008). Teaching disciplinary literacy to adolescents: Rethinking content-area literacy. *Harvard Educational Review, 78*(1), 40–59.

Siebert, D., & Draper, R. J. (2008). Why content-area literacy messages do not speak to mathematics teachers: A critical content analysis. *Literacy Research and Instruction, 47,* 229–245.

About the Contributors

Roni Jo Draper is an associate professor in the Department of Teacher Education in the David O. McKay School of Education at Brigham Young University, where she teaches courses in literacy methods and educational research. Her research interests include literacy and teacher education. Her publications focusing on content-area literacy have appeared in the *Harvard Educational Review*, the *American Educational Research Journal*, the *Journal of Literacy Research, Literacy Research and Instruction*, and the *Journal of Adolescent and Adult Literacy*. She currently is serving as Professional Materials Review Editor for the *Journal of Adolescent and Adult Literacy*.

Paul Broomhead is an associate professor in the School of Music at Brigham Young University, where he serves as the Coordinator of the Music Education Division. He has served in the National Association for Music Education as Chair of the Instructional Strategies Special Interest Research Group and as Western Division Collegiate Chair. He has published in the *Journal of Research in Music Education*, the *Bulletin of the Council for Research in Music Education, Music Educators Journal*, the *Journal of Music Teacher Education*, and *Update*. His teaching responsibilities include Exploration of Teaching, Philosophy of Music, Music Education Research, and Score Preparation/Conducting.

Amy Petersen Jensen is an associate professor in the College of Fine Arts and Communications at Brigham Young University, where she coordinates the undergraduate Theatre and Media Education Program as well as the Media Literacy Education Masters Degree Program. She is a past president of the Utah Theatre Association and the first vice president of the National Association for Media Literacy Education (NAMLE). She co-authored *Core Principles of Media Literacy Education in the United States*, NAMLE's position statement on media literacy education. She serves on the *Youth Theatre Journal* editorial board and is the co-editor of the *Journal of Media Literacy Education*.

Jeffery D. Nokes is an assistant professor in the History Department at Brigham Young University. He teaches a Methods of Teaching Social Studies course, supervises practicum students and student teachers, and teaches a World History course. Prior to his work at BYU, he taught world, United States, and Utah history in public schools. His work on literacy in history and social studies, methods of teaching social studies, and teacher education has been published in the *Journal of Educational Psychology*, the *Journal of Adolescent and Adult Literacy*, *Teaching and Teacher Education*, and the *National Social Science Journal*.

Daniel Siebert is an associate professor in the Department of Mathematics Education at Brigham Young University. His area of research is literacy and discourse in mathematics teaching and learning. His research has appeared in numerous publications in this field, including *Teaching Children Mathematics*, the *Journal of Mathematical Behavior*, *Literacy Research and Instruction*, and the *American Educational Research Journal*. He is an active member of the National Council of Teachers of Mathematics and a past associate editor of the *Journal for Research in Mathematics Education*.

Marta Adair is an associate teaching professor in the Biology Department at Brigham Young University, where she coordinates the biology-teaching program. She is responsible for the education programs at the BYU Monte L. Bean Life Science Museum and was the director of the Wetlands Education Project. In 2009 the Utah Science Teachers Association named her Outstanding University Science Educator.

Diane L. Asay has taught in the Art Education Department at Brigham Young University for over 18 years and has served as vice president of the National Art Education Association as well as president of the Utah Art Education Association.

Sharon R. Gray is an associate professor in the Visual Art Department at Brigham Young University. She is a J. Paul Getty Fellow in the Arts and a frequent presenter at the National Art Education Association and Utah Education Association. Her research recently was featured in a presentation at the 2008 International Society for Education Through Art World Congress in Osaka, Japan. Her background includes a decade as executive director of the Utah Statewide Art Partnership as well as associate director of the Springville Museum of Art. She served as president of the Utah Museum Association and of the Utah Art Education Association. She recently published in the *International Journal of Education Through Art*, the *Journal of Museum Education*, and *Curator: The Museum Journal*.

Sirpa Grierson is a associate professor and teaches education methods courses in the English Department at Brigham Young University. Currently she serves on the University Admissions Committee. Her research interests include classroom action research, multigenre writing, and adolescent literacy. A past president of the Utah Council of the International Reading Association, and currently vice president of the Utah Council of Teachers of English, she has served on national committees, including the International Reading Association Government Legislation Committee. Publications include articles in *Reading Research and Instruction*, the *English Journal*, *Language Arts*, and the *Journal of Adolescent and Adult Literacy*.

Scott Hendrickson is currently an assistant teaching professor in the Department of Mathematics Education at Brigham Young University, where he teaches methods courses to prospective secondary mathematics teachers and supervises their student teaching experiences. Previous to this assignment, Scott taught for 26 years in public education as a high school mathematics teacher.

Steven L. Shumway is an associate professor and chair of the Technology & Engineering Teacher Education Program in the School of Technology at Brigham Young University. He is an active member of the International Technology Education Association, past president of the Utah Trades & Technology Education Association, and a member of the National Center for Engineering and Technology Education. He has published in various journals, including *The Technology Teacher* and the *Council on Technology Teacher Education Yearbook*, and is a regular presenter at regional and national technology education conferences. His research interests include student motivation in the classroom and teaching robotics and engineering-related curriculum to K–12 students.

Geoffrey A. Wright is an assistant professor of Technology Engineering Education at Brigham Young University. His current areas of research and teaching include multimedia education, technology-enhanced teacher training, technology literacy, innovation design processes and creativity, professional learning communities, and the impact, development, and educational influence of emerging technologies. He is also chair of the TEE TECA student club and advises several student teachers each semester.

Index